Human Nature, Election, and History

Human Nature, Election, and History

by
WOLFHART PANNENBERG

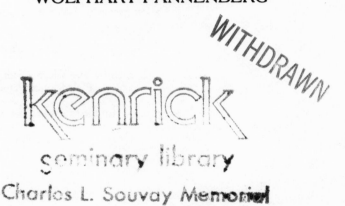

THE WESTMINSTER PRESS
Philadelphia

Scripture quotations from the Revised Standard Version
of the Bible are copyrighted 1946, 1952, © 1971, 1973
by the Division of Christian Education of the National
Council of the Churches of Christ in the U.S.A., and are
used by permission.

BOOK DESIGN BY DOROTHY ALDEN SMITH

First edition

Published by The Westminster Press®
Philadelphia, Pennsylvania

PRINTED IN THE UNITED STATES OF AMERICA

1 2 3 4 5 6 7 8 9

Library of Congress Cataloging in Publication Data

Pannenberg, Wolfhart, 1928–
    Human nature, election, and history.

    1. Man (Christian theology)   2. Kingdom of God.
3. Church and the world.   4. Election (Theology)—
History of doctrines.   5. History (Theology)
I. Title.
BT701.2.P34   233   77-22026
ISBN 0-664-24145-X

Contents

Preface

THE FIVE CHAPTERS PUBLISHED IN THIS VOLUME WERE DELIV-
ered as lectures at numerous seminaries and universities in the
United States and in Britain during fall and spring 1975–76.
The two chapters in Part One, "The Christian Idea of the
Human Person," were originally prepared for a Methodist min-
isters conference on "Resurgent Spirituality and Global Responsibility" at the School of Theology at Claremont, Califor-
nia. In the text of these chapters, traces of their relatedness to
the general subject of that conference will be recognized. The
main point is to restate the central importance of individual
existence in the perspective of the Christian faith, while at the
same time emphasizing the communal element of human destiny. This theme is related to the three chapters in Part Two,
"The Doctrine of Election and the History of Christianity,"
especially to their criticism of the abstract individualism in the
classical doctrine on election.

For this reason I decided to publish the five lectures together. Those on election were delivered as the Hoover Lectures at Chicago in January 1976 and also as the Ferguson
Lectures at the University of Manchester, England, in March
1976, as well as at a number of other places. In publishing these
lectures, I remember with gratitude the American and English
friends, students and colleagues, who made my visits to America and England a thoroughly enjoyable experience. I am especially indebted to Prof. Eckhart Mühlenberg, Prof. Robert

Wilken, Prof. Hans Hillerbrand, and Prof. Trutz Rendtorff for valuable advice that made my historical and systematic argument on election and history less vulnerable than it would otherwise have been. Docent Dr. Wolf-Dieter Hauschild, in connection with a joint seminar during the winter of 1973–74, brought to my attention some of the historical materials discussed in the fourth chapter.

WOLFHART PANNENBERG

Part One

THE CHRISTIAN IDEA
OF THE HUMAN PERSON

1
Human Nature
and the Individual

THE TRADITIONAL CHRISTIAN DOCTRINE ABOUT MAN DEVEL-
oped around two central ideas. One was the classical concept
of man as created in the image of God. The other was constituted by the notion of sin and referred back to the primordial
fall of Adam. But these two themes never exhausted the content of a Christian understanding of man. In fact, by themselves they do not even indicate the distinctively Christian
element in theological anthropology. The idea of man as
created in the image of God goes back to the Old Testament,
and so does the idea of human sinfulness. There have been
modifications, to be sure, of both ideas in Christian anthropology. But in order to appreciate these modifications, we have to
look first for what is distinctive in the Christian understanding
of man.

This distinctive element is to be found in the Christian
assertion that man has been reconciled to God in Christ. The
notion of reconciliation in Christ accounts for the modifications of the other two concepts in Christian thought. The
message that man has been reconciled to God in Christ would
lack universal significance if all men, without Christ, were not
actually constrained by the bondage of sin. The manifestation
of the universality of sin in the cross of Jesus is presupposed by
the universal salvation achieved by that event. The universality
of salvation, however, led to the assertion that only through
Christ does man reach his true destiny. If his being created in

the image of God indicates that divine destiny, it has been realized only in Christ and is now open to all men through him. Thus, it is finally the idea of reconciliation in Christ that constitutes the distinctively Christian perspective of human existence.

The Christian church, to the present day, claims general and universal validity for its message of reconciliation for all mankind in Christ. This claim has motivated the missionary activity of Christians and the spread of the Christian message all over the globe. But how is that claim to be substantiated? Why should people who do not feel their sinfulness long for reconciliation with God? The usual strategy of Christian missions has tended to avoid the seriousness of that question. Instead, people were told that there was only one true God who considers all men to be sinners against him, except for the work of Christ. Today we ask, however, whether this really is the true God, if there is any God at all. Do we have arguments to answer that question? Is there any criterion for judging the answers that are given? In my opinion, such a criterion can be found in the illuminative power of a given idea of God. The criterion is applied when we ask how a particular idea of God illuminates and has illuminated our understanding of reality and, especially, of human life. If God is the only origin and creator of man and his world, as his faithful followers claim, his revelation should provide a deeper and more comprehensive understanding of the content of our experience regarding man and his world.

Let us now apply this criterion to the Christian doctrine of man. How did the Christian understanding of man as reconciled with God in Christ in fact illuminate the human situation and the self-understanding of man in his world? What did the Christian message contribute to the way human beings experience themselves?

My thesis is that in a special sense *the eternal value of the individual and of his life* has been a most fundamental contribution of Christianity to the development and experience of the structure of human existence. This idea is a direct correlate of Jesus' proclamation of the reconciling love of God who searches for every single individual like a sheepholder who goes after the one sheep that is lost until he finds it. It is like the poor woman who turns everything in her house upside down until she finds the lost coin. It is like the father who rejoices in the return of his lost son. This image of God as searching with eternal love for every single individual gone astray attributed to the human individual an eternal value and dignity unheard of before.

Of course, this idea did not occur without preparation in history. It has its roots in ancient Jewish humanism and in Jewish history. One important precondition for its emergence was the belief in a future of the individual beyond his death as developed in postexilic Judaism. Before that time, no final importance had been attributed to the individual apart from involvement in the communal life of the people. Individual sin and failure did harm to the entire people, and individual righteousness was considered a source of blessing for all. The retribution and the rewards of the fathers were passed on to their posterity. The generation, however, that lived to see the destruction of Jerusalem by the Babylonians after the reign of the pious king Josiah could no longer recognize the righteousness of God in the course of history. Therefore Ezekiel proclaimed as a new provision of God: "The son shall not suffer for the iniquity of the father, nor the father suffer for the iniquity of the son; the righteousness of the righteous shall be upon himself, and the wickedness of the wicked shall be upon himself" (Ezek. 18:20).

Further experience, however, demonstrated that within the life span of many individuals the justice of God did not manifest itself adequately by the occurrence of punishments or rewards appropriate to the respective actions of individual men. To the contrary, there was widespread lamentation "that there are righteous men to whom it happens according to the deeds of the wicked, and there are wicked men to whom it happens according to the deeds of the righteous" (Eccles. 8:14). How could such experience be reconciled to the religious belief in the righteousness and justice of God? Challenged by such experience, Jewish faith in the righteousness of God came to believe in a further compensation by a life hereafter so that each individual finally would receive what was due according to his or her deeds. The early examples of Jewish belief in a resurrection of the dead show clearly the traces of their origin in the principle that God's righteousness is to be demonstrated in what happens to each individual. Therefore the emergence of the resurrection hope in postexilic Jewish faith definitively established and completed the emancipation of the individual from the social context in terms of possessing independent meaning and dignity. Of course, the individual continued to be held responsible for actions in the social context. The sense of such individual responsibility was even enhanced. But with the emergence of the resurrection hope the individual became an autonomous center of meaning in a way he had not been before.

To some extent, this development is comparable to the emergence of the idea of the immortality of the soul in Greek thought. The idea of an immortal soul also documents an emancipation of the individual from the social system. But if we look more closely, we see that the Platonic belief in the immortality of the soul did not attribute eternal value to the human individual. The soul is not identical with the individual, because the soul undergoes a series of successive reembodiments. Thus, the Jewish expectation of bodily resurrection emphasized far more the eternal importance of individual existence. In Jewish thought the individual is the place where God's righteousness is to be revealed, even beyond this present life. But even in Jewish thought the individual has not generally been conceived of as being the focus of concern of the eternal God himself as it was proclaimed by Jesus in his parables of the lost sheep, the lost coin, and the return of the lost son. In these parables, Jesus presented God as searching with eternal love for every single individual—not only for the righteous ones, but indeed especially for those who went astray. This demonstrated in an unmistakable way that God does not love men because of the intrinsic value of some individuals or because of their achievement. Rather, infinite value is attributed to people because of the eternal love of God for them.

Jesus' proclamation of God's love for every single individual was finally vindicated by his death on the cross. We need not go into detail here concerning the question of how the cross could be interpreted as the ultimate expression of God's love for the world. For the purpose of the present argument it is sufficient that in the light of Jesus' resurrection his death has been understood that way. That is the common point of all the different images used by early Christian interpretations of the cross. The most simple explanation is the Pauline one that communion with the crucified Christ establishes the hope of sharing also in his new life which has become manifest in his resurrection. Thus even death can no longer separate from the love of God those who have communion with Christ.

The consequences of this belief have been truly revolutionary. The foundations of the Roman Empire were shaken three centuries later because even the threat of a horrible death could no longer terrify Christians into renouncing their faith in Christ. The martyrs of the ancient church demonstrated to the world the freedom of the individual over against the society and the state because of the love of God revealed to them in the death of Christ. By the death of Christ the individual has become radically independent from any ultimate claims on his life by the society or the state.

This is the historical origin of what is known today as the principle of individual freedom. Since its religious foundations proved to be stronger than the power of the state, the political power had to accept it as a criterion and, if possible, as a new basis for a social system adapted to that principle. As we all know, this was no smooth process in history. First the church was accepted as a legitimate basis for the political order, since the message of the church was the source of the new freedom. Later the hierarchical structure of the church itself got into conflict with the Christian freedom which is rooted in the communion of the faithful with Christ. It is the tragic irony of Christian history that only the rupture of its ecclesiastical unity opened the way for the principle of individual freedom to become the ultimate criterion for the social system and for a degree of achievement in its political organization. In the wake of the confessional wars that shattered Europe for more than a century after the Reformation, the principle of individual freedom and the toleration of pluralism following from it had to be dissociated from its religious roots in the Christian faith. This step was necessary to establish a common basis for social life that was independent of the disastrous contest between mutually exclusive confessional interpretations of the Christian faith. Nevertheless, the emancipation of the principle of human freedom from its religious roots in the Christian faith has had tragic results. For Christianity, it led to the process of secularization in modern culture, with the consequence that religion has been progressively denied public validity and restricted to the private sphere of life. For modern culture, the isolation of the idea of individual freedom from religion has caused some of its basic values to become ambivalent and opaque because of the loss of their religious rootage.

The principle of individual freedom is not a self-evident fact of human nature. It is a liberal illusion that every man was born free, that limitations to our freedom have been imposed only from the outside, by the social system, and that all men would enjoy and peacefully live out their freedom if only those obstacles, those social limitations and inequalities, were removed. To be sure, this concept of a natural and primordial freedom of all men has been influential in Western thought—not only in modern times but for a long time before. It had been the thesis of Stoic philosophy that originally all men were free and equal by nature; the development of social relationships among men, it was thought, had produced inequalities and corrupted that primordial equality and freedom.

At this point a fundamental difference arises between the anthropology of Stoic philosophy and the Christian faith. The early Christians did not assume that men are free and equal by nature. Rather, they believed that men have to be liberated before they can be free. In the Gospel of John, Christ is reported to have said: "If the Son makes you free, you will be free indeed" (John 8:36). And Paul says (II Cor. 3:17): "Where the Spirit of the Lord is, there is freedom." In Paul, as in John, the Spirit of Christ is conceived of as a liberating power. Both favor a liberation theology. But it is not primarily a liberation from any oppressive social system that is needed so that a natural freedom of man can be exercised fully without crippling impediments. The human heart itself is considered the impediment. The Gospel of John puts it in a paradigmatic form. When Jesus promises them freedom, his audience tells him that they are not slaves. They feel themselves free already. But Jesus regards that as an illusion. Their behavior demonstrates that they are not free, because they want to kill him. Therefore, Jesus says: "Every one who commits sin is a slave to sin. The slave does not continue in the house for ever; the son continues for ever. So if the Son makes you free, you will be free indeed" (John 8:34–36).

This section from the Gospel of John represents a radical criticism of any belief in a natural freedom of man. Indeed, if men were free by nature, they would have no need of a savior. But since by their behavior they show themselves to be slaves to sin, they need liberation, liberation from their own sinfulness.

In later centuries, Christian theology accepted a compromise with Stoic principles. The Christians continued to affirm that man is not free by himself now, since he is a sinner. But they also asserted that the first man, Adam, in the state of his original innocence, was free in the way claimed by the Stoics for human nature. Thus, Christian anthropology could appear as a modified form of Stoicism. Eager to exonerate God by reference to the freedom of the first man from any responsibility for the irruption of sin and evil into his creation, Christian theology did in effect conceal the fundamental opposition between the Christian and the Stoic idea of freedom. Hence, also in modern thought the difference between the freedom granted by Christ and what was called the natural freedom of man often went unnoticed. To a large extent the ambiguities of modern liberalism are due to this fuzziness. A liberal may understand himself in continuity with the freedom granted by Christ and liberating man from the power of sin and death. But liberalism may also come down to nothing more than the Stoic idea of a natural freedom of man which, by New Testament standards, is to be considered an illusion.

From this basic illusion which is inseparable from the assumption that the original nature of man is good there follow all the other illusions of classical liberalism criticized so severely but aptly by Reinhold Niebuhr. There is especially the expectation that the uninhibited development of everybody's natural talents, needs, and desires will finally take place in harmony with everybody else's reasonable self-interest. Niebuhr noted that in some sense the assertion of a final identity of the particular with the common interest is correct, but it is never perfectly realized in a concrete situation. It is correct as an abstract ideal of reason, but the actual state of social affairs is dominated by the image of conflicting interests, of repression and rebellion. This is because it is so difficult to decide in the midst of conflicting interests what precisely the requirements of justice are, and, consequently, where the point of coincidence of the common interest with the true interest of the individual is located. The element of complacency in liberal attitudes is due to the fact that liberalism so often neglected the impact of sin in human life. Liberalism rarely considered the degree to which the appeal to reason and to the common good is subservient to the self-interest of individuals and groups. The results of this oversight have frequently been disastrous. Because the need for liberation from sin before man can be free in the full sense of the word has not been taken very seriously by liberalism, the connection between religion and human freedom has been almost obliterated. In turn, the liberal idea of freedom has become so shallow that it is open to easy criticism. Especially it has been blamed, by Marx and his followers, for its formalism, for its abstraction from the actual social situation of individuals who because of their social condition are not in a position to claim for themselves the possibilities which formally should be open to everybody. Therefore it is doubtful whether people who are considered to be free in a formal and legal sense are actually in possession of their freedom.

There is another side to that formalism of the liberal idea of freedom. Even where the right to choose is fully exercised, it still remains doubtful whether the individual person is free in the authentic sense of the word. The liberal principle of freedom can be judged as depriving individuals of a meaningful life precisely by leaving them to their own more or less badly informed or manipulated choice. If despite all these difficulties individual freedom is to be considered essential to human dignity, it is finally a religious judgment. Thus Hegel may have been right, after all, in tracing back the modern principle of individual freedom to the Christian faith, since, as he said, the Christian faith assured the individual of his unity with the absolute truth. This judgment does not mean that the Christian faith was the only element, in terms of the history of ideas, from which the modern idea of freedom came. We have mentioned the importance of Stoic ideas to the rise of the modern principle of liberty. But, despite Stoic natural law, for nearly two thousand years people did not effectively claim the principle of equal individual freedom as a basis for actual political life. This step was taken for the first time in Protestant Christianity after the Reformation had insisted upon the immediacy of the individual Christian to Christ as the constitution of the freedom of his faith that renders him in his own conscience independent from all human authority.

Even Protestant Christianity, however, did not take spontaneously the step toward a political realization of the principle of Christian freedom. Luther considered it as a matter of only the inward life of the individual person. The radical claim to the exclusive validity of religious truth and the concern for the religious unity of the social unit stood in the way of a religious pluralism adequate to the Christian idea of individual freedom. Only the impasse of the confessional wars forced upon the political system the concession to pluralism. Once that had occurred, however, it could be legitimated as representing the true consequence of the Christian idea of freedom. This is the decisive point. The legitimation of pluralism in the free exercise of individual freedom could not be given simply on the basis of natural law, since it had been agreed upon for a long time that the provisions of natural law are not directly applicable to the present situation of social life. Therefore, the Christian experience of freedom from sin and death by communion with Christ was the indispensable basis for claiming the principles of natural law for the task of reshaping the structure of social life after the confessional wars and throughout the modern period. Without the Christian experience of individual freedom in being united to the absolute reality of God, the ideas of natural law had continued to function as pure abstractions. And without that religious basis and content they function even today as pure abstractions, fraught with all the dangers and injustices of mistaking the abstract for the concrete.

This is particularly evident in the idea of equality which is intrinsic to individual freedom, if freedom is understood not as freedom for some individuals in contrast to others but as freedom for human individuals as such. Equality as a principle of natural law, however, is difficult to apply to a concrete case of human relations. In their concrete life, human individuals are neither equal nor equally free, and these inequalities cannot be attributed altogether to different opportunities and social conditions. Yet all individuals participate even now in a common destiny of being human, and this constitutes a deeper equality among them despite all their inequalities. As a result, there is a delicate balance in the social life of human individuals between their *natural inequality* and their *proleptic equality*. Their proleptic, or anticipated, equality derives from their common destiny and is closely related to their dignity as persons. It is the difficult task of social policy to do justice to both sides, to the actual inequality and to the proleptic equality of the citizen. If the actual inequalities are neglected, a totalitarian idealism is at work that distorts the concrete facts of life.

If, however, the proleptic equality of man is disregarded, the humane criterion for social reform is surrendered.

Our discussion of the Christian concept of individual freedom and of the modern concept of freedom, which is based predominantly on the ideas of natural law, leads to the conclusion that the two are not mutually exclusive, at least not necessarily so. But there are strong tensions between them. The Christian idea of freedom is not formalistic and abstract. It has a particular content, i.e., the communion of the believer with God, who in Christ prevailed over the power of sin and death and thus reconciled man to himself. What the two concepts of freedom have in common is that freedom belongs to the essence of being human. It is understandable to the Christian that others also, including the Stoic philosophers, had some idea of freedom, if only in the form of a faint abstraction. But the idea of freedom does not belong only to the essence of being human; it points to the way that essence is present in human existence. Here, however, the deepest difference between the Christian view and secular liberalism is located. In the Christian perspective, the general condition of human existence means that man is alienated from himself. In the midst of his alienation man may still know about freedom, but he regards as freedom what is in fact his alienated existence, and that demonstrates more clearly than anything else his alienation. The alienated man may have an idea of freedom, but he enjoys no real freedom. In a Christian perspective, real freedom is communicated to man only by his reconciliation to God in Christ.

The historical character of the Christian experience of freedom has its impact on the understanding of human nature. In the light of this experience the term "nature" becomes ambivalent. It includes two elements: the actual character, and the true essence of a thing. If the essence of human life were to be found in the way human beings normally behave, the two elements would coincide. But if the essence of human life includes what is not always realized (such as freedom is not realized except by the mediation of the particular historical

event), then the essence of being human in comparison to the
general condition of human existence belongs to a dimension
of a "not yet" which nevertheless determines the present even
now. The present life of human individuals even in the case of
radical alienation is still human. The essence or essential nature
of being human thus becomes a matter of the destiny of men
to be human, in contrast to the natural conditions and character of their behavior. Human nature, then, is no longer some
given and invariable structure, but has a history. More precisely, human nature *is* the history of the realization of human
destiny. In Biblical terms, man is the history from the first
Adam to the second Adam, who, according to Paul, has become manifest in Jesus Christ and especially in the new life of
his resurrection. That in Jesus Christ the destiny of man is
realized—although not yet in its universal efficacy for all men
—was expressed in Biblical language by calling Christ the
image of God. According to the Old Testament, man was
created to be the image of God, so that this constitutes the
essential nature of man. In early Christian theology, however,
it is only in Jesus Christ and through him that the image of
God is realized in mankind. Therefore, the remark in the first
chapter of Genesis that man was created "in" the image of
God has been interpreted in Christian theology to mean that
the nature of man was constituted by relating him to the image
of God connected with his destiny manifest in Jesus Christ.

This Christological interpretation of the old Israelite concept of the distinctive nature of man as being created in the
image of God has consequences regarding the content of that
idea. According to the Old Testament, its meaning was that
within the entire creation, man represents the sovereignty of
God over against the other creatures on earth. "Fill the earth
and subdue it" (Gen. 1:28). In recent years this divine mandate
has been made responsible for the ruthless exploitation of nature by Western man that now threatens ecological disaster.
But such blame is somewhat unfair, since the meaning of the
divine mandate was not that man should treat other creatures
at his will, but that he should act as the deputy of the creator.

This could hardly mean permission to destroy his creation. However this may be, if the destiny of man to act in the image of God has been realized only in Christ, then the meaning of the dominion entrusted to man becomes even more specific. The rule of Christ consists in reconciling to God what had been separated from God. The ministry of Jesus Christ, to be sure, is directed to mankind and not to minerals or plants or animals. Nevertheless we have to think about the cosmological dimension of his rule along the same line. The realization of the image of God in Jesus Christ calls for responsible steward-ship of man in the creation which, in the words of Paul, "waits with eager longing" for "the glorious liberty of the children of God" (Rom. 8:19–21).

The problems of ecology point once more to the difference between the Christian and the secular concept of freedom. The Christian idea of man as commissioned to act in the image of God places him near God, as Jewish faith does, over against the rest of the world. This constitutes the element of indepen-dence in his freedom. There is no room for devotion to nature. But neither is there a license for treating God's creation at will.

The connection between the Christian experience of free-dom and the Christian interpretation of the Jewish concept of man as created in the image of God serves to express the universal significance of that experience. The liberation from the power of sin and death to the enjoyment of freedom in communion with God is not meant only for the Christians as the happy few. It is meant for the whole world. Especially it is meant for the whole of mankind. By his ministry, death, and resurrection Jesus communicated the freedom of the children of God to those who trust in him. But far beyond this circle a light is thrown by Jesus' history upon every human being. Every individual is called to the freedom communicated through Jesus Christ. That means liberation from the power of sin and death and consists in peace with God. In the light of Jesus' history every human being is destined to that personal independence. This does not necessarily justify so-called libera-tion movements. All too often they delude the people, and sometimes themselves also, by using the human yearning for freedom as an instrument for the rise to power of another political elite. But the light of the love of God resting on every human individual denies to the political authorities of any sort the right to dispose of human individuals at will. The victims of oppression and exploitation can at least know that and remain independent in their conscience.

The line of this argument may sound like a legitimation of individualism, but it is not. The individual is not considered the final authority for his or her own life. Here again we have to remember the difference between modern liberalism and the Christian idea of freedom. The image of the individual who takes himself or herself to be the center of his or her life aptly describes the structure of sin. In Augustine's analysis, egocentricity underlies the structure of concupiscence. Concupiscence must not be narrowed down to sexuality, but denotes the formal structure of judging everything primarily by the standard of whether it is of advantage or disadvantage to one's own person. In the Christian tradition this radical individualism is considered as alienation from the authentic destiny of man. When the highest value is no longer universal reason, but individual decision, radical autonomy has been often considered the peak of existential freedom. In a Christian perspective, it can be the darkest alienation from authentic existence, from one's own destiny and identity. Individual life needs a standard beyond oneself that is not at one's own disposal. Only in this way can it obtain substantial content and meaning. Lest one surrender the promise of freedom, the reality which is radically and completely beyond one's own disposal should be only God. Entrusting oneself completely to any other would amount to idolatry. Because of his communion with God, however, and by participation in God's love to the world, the individual who entrusts himself to God will also serve his fellowmen on their way toward their divine destiny.

Thus the Christian emphasis on the individual person does not mean individualism. Therefore the Christian should not go in for the pretended right of everybody to develop and realize all his natural potential and desires. There is much in human nature that has to be overcome. Perhaps it should not simply be suppressed, because then it gets out of control. But our natural tendencies certainly need to be disciplined and civilized. The consequence is that the desires of men and their claims are often not identical with, but are sometimes contrary to, their actual needs. But who can make the distinction and by what criterion? At this point authorities emerge who would do away with personal autonomy altogether. The question also arises about the function of religion not only in individual life but also in the structure of societies. It depends on the kind of religion whether it allows for the final value of individual life and consequently for pluralism of behavior and opinion.

2

The Social Predicament
and Human Responsibility

EVERY INTERPRETATION OF JESUS' MESSAGE HAS TO DO JUSTICE
to the fact that Jesus was concerned for individual persons in
their personal relations to God. Yet his message was not a
matter of private devotion. He proclaimed the Kingdom of
God to come, and with that proclamation he stood in the
tradition of the political expectations of the Jewish people.
These expectations were concentrated on the hope for a social
order of peace and justice. But since the time of the prophets
this order had not been expected to come about as a result of
any change in human rule or in the structure of government.
It could come only from the rule of God himself replacing all
forms of government by men over other men. Perhaps this
Jewish realism concerning the character of all human government helps to explain why Jesus proclaimed the Kingdom of
God to come in such a surprisingly personal, almost private
form. In any case, he did not join those who called for revolution of the social order or for liberation from the Roman
occupation. Obviously he did not expect that any such revolution would bring about the Kingdom that he came to proclaim.
Nevertheless, in his peculiar way, he continued the political
expectations of Israel. This implies that the destiny of man not
only is a matter of his private life but involves the political
community also. Therefore the Christian has to accept responsibilities beyond the narrow circle of his private life. But what
kind of responsibilities are at stake?

Before answering that question, we should first appreciate the peculiar reserve in Jewish prophetism concerning the possibilities of political action and organization. What understanding of the human situation in the world is implied in the prophets' increasingly pessimistic outlook concerning human government? To bring about peace and justice constitutes the primary task of every form of political order. Why, then, was it the judgment of Jewish faith that only God himself and no human government can successfully attain that objective? What anthropological presuppositions are implied in this judgment?

If we think of the prophetic criticism directed against the kings of Israel and Judah, the striking fact is that those personalities were addressed by the prophets without regard to the glamour of their high office. They were seen simply as human persons with their individual inclinations and limitations. This precisely is the problem. Those who exercise political power are in charge of the common interest of society. They act in behalf of the people. They have to carry through what the commonweal requires against the particularism of individuals or groups. Still, their own individual inclinations, preferences, and interests are never completely separable from their office. Therefore, the subjects not only feel the challenge to subordinate themselves to the commonweal but they also grumble at the arbitrary, prejudiced, and one-sided behavior of those in political office. In some cases this may be little more than an excuse for individualistic stubbornness. Nevertheless it explains why tensions always remain between the individual and society, tensions which from time to time turn into open conflict.

Therefore, as long as the common cause of the society is to be administered by individual persons over against other individual persons, peace and justice will not definitively be secured. Although restrictions imposed upon political power may help a great deal, situations of rebellion and repression will continue to occur. Since only the reign of God himself will put an end to the rule of men over other men, peace and justice will be perfectly realized only in the Kingdom of God. This also explains why Jesus did not call for political action in order to further the arrival of God's Kingdom. Although God's Kingdom will bring the realization of man's political destiny—a life in peaceful communion with all other men—it cannot be furthered but can only be distorted by any attempt to attain that goal by direct political action. Programs to that effect are inevitably delusive. Jesus was not a zealot.

We now understand better why Jesus concentrated his proclamation of God's imminent Kingdom on the individual. But even so, his message involved the idea of an eschatological community, of a new humanity under God. The love of God, the creator and redeemer of the world, is extended to all human beings. One can stay in communion with God only by participating in his love for the world. Thus, God's love aims at a universal community of human beings in communion with him. At present, this eschatological community is represented and symbolized by the community of the faithful. They serve the same function that was intended for the chosen people of Israel. The election of Israel was aimed at the blessing of all mankind, and this vocation continues. When Jesus chose twelve disciples to follow him, they were to represent the twelve tribes of Israel, an eschatologically renewed Israel that would be faithful to its calling. This indicates the continuity between the chosen people of Israel and the Christian church. The church is not the "new Israel" as if the old one were no longer God's elected people. The church is an extension of the election of Israel, including within its community members from all nations. In this way, the election of Israel is continued; the Christian church symbolizes the eschatological universalism of the Kingdom of God.

These matters had to be mentioned because the communion of the faithful as a symbolic representation of the imminent Kingdom of God constitutes the alternative to the devious attempt to establish the divine Kingdom by political action. Human beings cannot force the coming of the Kingdom; they can only respond themselves to the call of God's future and symbolize it in the present world. The community of the church symbolizes the eschatological Kingdom of a new mankind in communion with God. Even the Christian churches today continue to fulfill to some degree this symbolic function in spite of their divisions. But their divisions severely obscure and distort that function. Therefore the churches are badly in need of radical reform according to their divine mission in this world.

We have now seen how the universalism of the Kingdom of God points beyond the private life of the individual. It has become apparent how in the life of the political community its destiny toward the Kingdom of God is effective, but also how this effectiveness is broken by the ambiguities of human government. Therefore the destiny of an eschatological community of all mankind under God can be symbolized at present only by the community of the faithful. This community, however, is not a mere sign, but is an effective sign and symbol of the Kingdom. In proportion to the degree to which the church symbolizes the Kingdom, while distinguishing itself from it, the Kingdom as the future destiny of man becomes present in the church. The church thus becomes an effective sign of the Kingdom, effective precisely by way of a symbol and not otherwise.

In order to explore this further, some reflections on the relations between the church and the political order are pertinent. The very existence of the church as a separate institution indicates the provisional character of the political order. There would be no need for the church as a separate religious institution if the social destiny of man to a life in communion with all other men were adequately implemented by the political order. This follows from the political character of the Kingdom of God: In the New Jerusalem there will be no temple anymore, no separate religious institution, because God will be in the midst of his people. They will be united with him and by him.

Therefore the separate existence of religion and of the church as a religious institution indicates, as Karl Marx stated correctly, that the essence of what it means to be human has

not yet been fully realized. However, as we took into consideration before, the common destiny of man cannot be realized by
the political order of society without the abrogation of some
form of government of men over men. Marx understood this
to be the case, but he was not fully aware that some form of
government of men over men in all political systems established by human political action is inevitable. History has since
demonstrated that this is not a question of economic revolution. The countries that experienced a socialist revolution in
our century developed a stronger state than most other countries. The promise that state and political government would
wither away after the socialist revolution has gone unfulfilled.

This experience of our age documents once again that only
the Kingdom of God will do away with the lordship of men
over men. Religion, far from having lost its function and illuminative power for human life, is confirmed again in pointing to
the only radical solution for the problems of social life and
political order. Thus the very existence of religion and of a
separate religious institution like the church testifies to the
provisional character of any man-made form of the social and
political order. The Christian church has done so self-con-
sciously by continuously persisting in its separate existence over
against the political order. This need not require what we call
in modern times the separation between church and state.
Even in periods of Christian history when the state was reor-
ganized on the basis of the Christian faith, the church continued to exist as a separate institution. The bishops never
became merely the agents of the state, although the identification of Christians and of their bishops with their particular
political unit often went too far. This happened not only in
Byzantium but even more so in the history of modern nationalism. Only the international unity of the church catholic offers
a reliable remedy against that temptation. In any case, the
church should remind political systems of all kinds of their
provisional nature. The church does so by its very existence.
But it should also press this point by the actions of its officers
and bishops in situations of crucial importance. The testimony

to the provisional nature of the political order is part of the fundamental contribution of the church to society at large. But certainly this negative contribution of the church to society has to be complemented by actions of equally symbolic character, actions that testify to God's promise of peace and justice, of aiding the poor and feeding the hungry.

The difference between the church and the state does not necessarily entail separation in the modern sense. The issue of the religious neutrality of the state and of its dissociation from any accountability to particular religious institutions arose historically as a consequence of the confessional wars after the time of the Reformation. Religious neutrality of the state is, to be sure, an illusion. No political order is able to secure the loyalty of its people without legitimating itself by calling upon some highest truth that supposedly is beyond human manipulation. But in spite of the illusory character of the concept of religious neutrality of the state, the issue of separation between state and churches was historically unavoidable. The fanatic antagonism of confessional loyalties had almost destroyed the basis for social life.

Modern societies as well as the churches had to pay a price for the policy of separation. The increasing and largely unrecognized influence of civil religions, especially of nationalism, in so-called Christian countries, was the price paid for the illusion of a religious neutrality of the state. The restriction of traditional Christian religion to the level of a private conviction suppressed awareness of the inevitably religious foundation of social life. It has forced this dimension of social life into a nonreligious, secular camouflage. And to a large extent it deprived the Christian churches of their specific function concerning the political order. In most Western countries the state, in spite of its separation from the churches, continued to understand itself to be in some continuity with Christian values. The churches rarely took the step of exposing the self-glorification of a political order that no longer recognized itself as provisional over against symbolic authority of the church. How, then, is the public responsibility of the Christian to be exercised? Are the churches unnecessary for that purpose?

Similar problems arise in modern times in relation to other partial systems of the society. I shall confine my discussion to one more example: the economy. In modern times, economic tendencies, as long as they did not come into conflict with politics, were made independent, especially in the high period of liberalism. I regard this development as concomitant with the dissociation of the political order from traditional religion. The autonomy of the state and the autonomy of economic development have been twins. The consequence was the almost physical necessity and apparent inevitability in the development of modern capitalism as it was described by Karl Marx. I regard his general thesis of the primacy of the economic factor in historical processes as an extrapolation of what in reality happened only in modern capitalism. It happened here on the basis of the privatization of religion after the end of the confessional wars. The economic process, so to speak, got out of hand, and to this day we struggle against the consequences.

All these developments concerning the relations between church and society, its political and economic order, have to be in view when we ask today what are the human responsibilities of the Christian beyond the limits of his or her private life. The question as to the function of the church is not a side issue. In fact, it is the key to the problem. If it belongs to the essence of the Christian faith that there be a community of Christians, then the public responsibility of a Christian as a member of that community, his global responsibility for mankind, is represented by the church. Whether it is represented badly or well depends not only on the actions of church officials but on the structure of the church or churches, which in turn conditions the actions to be taken. Therefore, the first question to be asked should be: Does the structure of the church or churches adequately express their symbolic function for the eschatological unity of mankind in the Kingdom of God? Only then will the actions of the church be understood appropriately. At least they will be more easily understood in their symbolic meaning, and not only in terms of extraordinary miracles of the Holy

Spirit. The symbolic meaning of the church and of the church's actions in the global perspective of mankind cannot be understood adequately, however, without the unity of all Christian churches in the one church catholic which is the body of Christ. Without this context, some of the most valuable activities of the churches—for example, the work of Bread for the World—are in danger of losing their symbolic meaning. They become just one humanitarian activity alongside others, or even become identified with different religiopolitical motivations as, for example, so-called liberation movements.

Whether or not the structure of the churches together with their actions expresses adequately the global responsibility of the Christian faith is a matter of interest for all Christians and not only for our particular religious tradition. If the Christian faith has something to do with the destiny of man as such, then the symbolic function of the church is essential for the realization of human personality. The freedom of the individual person is mediated historically by the church, and especially by the distinction between church and state. This implies the provisional nature of the state, the freedom of the individual over against the political authorities, and, at the same time, the citizenship of the individual in a universal community of man in the Kingdom of God symbolically represented by the church. The presence of the Christian church in history witnesses to a community of men other than that which is realized by the political systems of social life that rely upon human organization and control.

The responsibility of the Christian is, in short, to assist other persons (as opportunity permits) in their realization of their human destiny, in their becoming human beings in the full sense of existing in the image of God. This responsibility, however, is carried out in different ways. The main difference lies between the personal sphere of direct person-to-person encounter and the global responsibility for people whom we do not personally encounter at all. I need not speak here about the forms of Christian responsibility in personal relations. In contrast to this field, global responsibility is always mediated by institutions. The most important of these institutions are, for our purpose, the churches and the political community. In addition, there are voluntary associations. They usually work within the political community or in connection with the churches. In some cases they also work as independent institutions or on an international level. I shall not dwell on their contribution, but limit the following discussion to the church and the state.

Our earlier reflections on the relations between church and political order permit now a somewhat differentiated description of the global responsibility implicit in the Christian faith. This responsibility should be assumed in the first place by the Christian church. We have to consider, however, the particular character of the church as a symbolic (or spiritual) institution. The relationship of the history of Christ and of the Christian faith to mankind at large is primarily symbolic. Correspondingly, the relationship of the church to mankind is also primarily of a symbolic nature. This does not mean, of course, that these relationships to all mankind have no reality. That Christ died for all men and that with the Kingdom of God the universality of a new mankind is in some way present already in the church are to be taken as reality, according to the Christian faith. But these realities are mediated by the symbolic significance of the cross of Jesus and of the contribution of the church.

The assertion that the relationship of the church to mankind at large is primarily symbolic stands in apparent contradiction to the commission of the resurrected Lord at the end of the Gospel of Matthew: "Go therefore and make disciples of all nations" (Matt. 28:19). This has been understood as a commission to convert all human individuals and thus all the nations on earth, all mankind, to the Christian faith. In our time this has become a debated issue. Do we really have to baptize everybody? Obviously Christian missions have somewhat fallen short of that mark. Does this failure demonstrate that, after all, Christ is not given all authority on earth? Or did some misunderstanding occur concerning his commission? Confronted by such alternatives, a Christian will be inclined to choose the second. Indeed, a misunderstanding is at hand if the effort toward conversion is taken as the primary form of how the church is related to mankind. This view leads to an imperialistic conception of Christian missions. The situation is different if one recognizes that the primary relationship of the church to mankind is symbolic in that the church celebrates in its liturgy the anticipation of the Kingdom of God, the community of the new mankind under God in praising his glory. The more this symbolic nature of the church becomes apparent, the more people will be attracted to the church and come to be taught and baptized. To this extent, there is no contradiction to the commission of Christ.

The primary relationship of the church to mankind at large is a symbolic witness borne by the church in its very existence. All actions and declarations of the church concerning mankind should take place in accordance with this symbolic (or sacramental) character of the nature of the church. This applies to its teaching, liturgy, assemblies and offices, to its ecumenical and missionary activities, and to the church's charity in feeding the hungry and aiding the poor and oppressed. These last-mentioned activities are also symbolic in character, as Jesus' activities of healing and feeding people were. The church cannot settle the general problem of hunger on earth. That is a task of the political order and of the community of nations. It is not a task of the church, although the Christian conscience is tempted to see it that way. Of Christ it is said that he rejected the challenge to convert rocks into bread in order to satisfy all hunger in the world. Should his church take the line that he rejected as a temptation? A highly questionable method in modern missionary work was to attract people to the church by offering them material advantages. This could even amount to bribing them into being converted. However, if the church, in granting material help, makes all connection with the Christian faith invisible, then the church is acting like any other humanitarian institution. It does not live up to its particular responsibility for mankind which requires the witness to the

Kingdom of God as mediated by Jesus Christ.

Of course, the commandment of love and the Golden Rule demand help for those who are in need. Although both of these imperatives are concerned with personal relations and not with institutions, on the level of institutional activities the question of justice is closely related. A justice that transcends and transforms the legal system thus manifests itself as an expression of love. Justice is the subject of the political organization of societies. Thus, as a member of a politically organized society, the Christian will accept responsibility for what happens to people in other parts of the world. Individual Christians as well as the Christian churches in a given country urge their political authorities to accept such responsibilities. This may have contributed to a large extent to the fact that most countries today regard some such responsibilities as mandatory. To be sure, there is a difference between the internal affairs of a given state and its foreign relations. The principle of justice does not constitute a title for interference with the internal affairs of another state. However, one may ask whether a case of strictly internal affairs could be claimed where fundamental human rights are involved. The question is debated. Fortunately, in cases when the principle of justice requires humanitarian help for people in foreign countries, few governments object to receiving it. They may, however, claim the right to distribute such help themselves, or at least to cooperate in its distribution. An additional difficulty is that nations in their foreign policy tend to seek their own advantage even in granting help to others. This is especially true of the modern secular state. These ambiguities are often felt and sometimes resented by those nations which received help for their own development.

In this particular situation an additional responsibility has imposed itself upon the churches. It is the task of acting vicariously for the political community of nations that should take care of securing fundamental standards of human life all over the world. The present condition of the United Nations demonstrates that such a community of nations is still far from being realized. In such a situation, the churches may assume certain vicarious functions which ordinarily should be performed by the community of nations. In a similar way the churches throughout their history occasionally accepted responsibilities that normally belonged to the political community. They were performed vicariously by the church in periods of political disruption or in other situations when the political authorities failed to meet their human responsibilities. In this way I understand certain forms of ecclesiastical development aid and other activities of the World Council of Churches. There are, of course, dangers at hand. Such an interecclesiastical organization may arrogate to itself an authority that it does not legally possess. In such a case the judgments and decisions of such an institution become easily suspect. They may be seen as partisan, or as not representative of the churches behind them, or not symbolically representative of the Kingdom of God. This danger is closely connected with the division of the churches. There is in the Protestant world no institution that would be authorized to speak for the churches. The global responsibility of the churches, however, which induced the churches to ecumenical cooperation, requires the further step of church unity and of an office representing the universal church. The absence of full ecclesiastical unity and of an institution representing the universal church in a period of institutionalized cooperation of the churches almost necessitates the arrogation of that representative function by agencies responsible for such cooperation.

This leads to the strategy I want to advocate for the Christian churches in facing their global responsibility. In all the sections of divided Christianity, Christians should concentrate their efforts on rediscovering the constitutive importance of the church for their identity as Christians. The church, in this sense, is primarily understood not as a particular community but as the universal community of all who confess Christ. It is the church catholic which we confess to in the Apostolic Creed and which is present in the liturgy of each local community. Whether contemporary Christianity lives up to its global responsibility better than former generations of Christians so

that it may effectively symbolize and testify within history to
the final destiny of man depends on producing a new visibility
of the body of Christ. It depends on the future of the ecumenical cause. I am deeply convinced that everything that could be
done by the churches to meet the global responsibility of Christianity, as long as it postpones overcoming our inherited divisions, will remain radically ambiguous and probably not be very
effective. It will inevitably lack most of the inspirative power
of Christian symbolism. I am afraid the time has passed when
the divided churches were still credible to some degree as *the*
church. There can be no Christian identity without the
church. Individualism is not a Christian option. But neither
can there be an authentic church without Christian unity. This
could largely explain why so many Christians continue to live
in the absurd fashion of a Christian individualism.

Within the broad spectrum of Christian denominations,
there are certainly some that need less than others to be re-
minded of the constitutive importance of the church for Christian identity. The problem is most acute in the Protestant
churches. But the Orthodox and Roman Catholic churches
seem often too quick to identify their churches exclusively as
the one catholic church, although today most of them no
longer deny other Christians the claim to be members of the
body of Christ. The Protestant churches have an important
element to contribute to a new realization of Christian unity:
the element of pluralism.

Today it is possible to conceive of pluralism, not as opposed
to any given theological interpretation of the Christian faith,
but as a consequence of a more adequate understanding of
God's revelation in Christ. The importance of eschatology for
all the particular subject matters in theology alerted theologians to recognize the element of the "not yet" in the descrip-
tions of the present situation of the Christian given in the New
Testament. This applies also to the situation and structure of
the church that is still looking forward to the future of God to
come. From this the element of pluralism follows. It is closely
related to the provisional character of Christian life in the
situation of pilgrimage. Even our knowledge of God's revela-

tion is still provisional and therefore allows for different inter-pretations. This justification of pluralism on the basis of God's revelation also indicates its limitation. But it offers a key notion for keeping together the elements of unity and pluralism. And it produces far-reaching consequences. First, it provides neces-sary space for the Christian freedom of the individual in con-trast to dogmatic uniformity, but without any loss of his or her Christian identity. Secondly, the recognition of the provisional nature of the present institutional form of the church provides a basis for a better understanding and mutual acknowledgment of different church traditions, theological perspectives, and ecclesiastical structures. Thirdly, the recognition of the provi-sional character of our Christian life and knowledge of God's revelation changes our attitude toward non-Christian religions. There is no longer the simple opposition between truth and falsehood. We can recognize in the adherents of other religions a search for the same divine mystery that we came to know as the God of Israel and of Jesus Christ, even if others cannot see it that way now. This attitude is more than toleration. It represents a new and contemporary form of Christian humility and even induces the Christian to learn from other religious traditions. If this change in the attitude toward others becomes dominant among Christians, it should reduce the suspicions directed against efforts for a reunification of the Christian churches. A new ecclesiastical manifestation of the catholic unity of all the disciples of Christ is possible today only on the basis of that pluralism which results from the appreciation of the eschatological and historical character of God's revelation and of the Christian faith. Such a pluralistic church will consti-tute no threat to the adherence of other religious traditions in terms of pressure or hostility. Such a church will present itself instead as a basis for cooperation. It will rely for its missionary activity upon the Spirit of Christ working through the symbolic (and sacramental) presence of the church, illuminating the individual existence of men and women as well as their social life, thus assuring them of their individual freedom as well as of their social destiny in the context of mankind.

Part Two

THE DOCTRINE OF ELECTION
AND THE HISTORY OF CHRISTIANITY

3
Election and the People of God

IN MODERN CHRISTIAN THOUGHT THE PROBLEM OF THE REAL-
ity of God has become increasingly intricate. The reasons for
this development may be found first in the fact that the idea
of God lost its function in explaining nature because of the rise
of classical physics and secondly in the criticism of the idea of
God and of religious consciousness in modern philosophy and
atheism. But the devastating impact of this criticism on Christian confidence in the reality of God requires additional explanatory factors.

One of them can be identified in the difficulty of perceiving
God as active in history, in our history. Of course, we learn that
the God of Israel was the God who acts. Biblical writings tell
us much about God's activity in the history of ancient Israel.
That God acted in Jesus has been accepted all along by the
faithful Christian. But right after the end of the early Christian
period, apparently, a purely secular history began to develop.
Since the early second century, if we listen to modern church
historians, there has been no action of God. Such a presentation causes serious problems, especially for a Christian understanding of modern times and of the contemporary world. A
God who does not act at all simply is no God. He would be
powerless and thus a nonentity. Consequently, the Biblical
reports on God's actions in history seem to represent nothing
more than some old-fashioned view of reality, a view that the
enlightened realism of our time has outgrown.

My suspicion is, however, that the sense of God's action in history has been lost in consequence of a one-sided development in the doctrine of election. This, at least, may be part of an explanation. In the Old Testament, the notion of election —together with that of God's promise—provided the key to understanding what happened to the Jewish people in terms of actions of their God. In connection with a number of additional elements to be discussed later, the idea of election constituted a framework of a theology of history. Such a theology of history assigned to each present generation its place in God's design for all mankind. Thus, an interpretation of one's own historical experience in terms of God's action in history became possible. Even in such a perspective, historical experience offers puzzling and obscure occurrences. But on the basis of the ancient Israelite concept of election, at least in principle it was possible to recognize in the course of events the action of God. With modern Christianity, however, this has become extremely difficult. The notion of election ceased to function as a key to history. One reason for its disappearance is that long before in the official doctrine of the church the notion of election had been detemporalized and individualized. It continued to be vigorous in somewhat unofficial forms of Christian consciousness, but in modern times Christian religious language more and more ceased to function as an important instrument in public discourse.

The classical doctrine of election, as represented in the work of Thomas Aquinas and Calvin, offers little reference to history. Instead, it deals with an eternal decision of God, made before the creation, and (usually) relates immediately to individuals concerning their final salvation. Three elements characterized this classical doctrine of election: the timelessness of the divine decision in regard to its subject, the restriction of its objects to individuals (in most cases to unrelated individuals), and finally the predominance of a transcendent salvation as constituting the purpose decided upon in the act of election. These elements characterized the classical concept both in its strictly Augustinian and in its more or less Semi-Pelagian form.

Subordinate to the concept of election occurs the notion of predestination. It deals with the means that God considers adequate for guiding the elected one on his way toward his preordained goal, eternal salvation—or, in the negative case, to eternal damnation. Instead of functioning as a subordinate concept, however, predestination has also been regarded as the more comprehensive term, with election as its nucleus or principle. In each case, the notion of predestination in some way reintroduces history into the doctrine of election. Because predestination starts with the internal decision of election, however, it is a predetermined process that lacks the most important characteristic of history, contingency. The following discussion will disregard these further complications connected with the concept of predestination in order to concentrate on the idea of election that provided the basis for the classical doctrine.

Since in the classical doctrine the object of election, the individual person, is presented in abstraction from any social and temporal context, it shall be called the "abstract" concept of election. In contrast to it, the early Old Testament notion of election was primarily related to the people of God. There is, to be sure, some mention also of individuals' being elected, but only as taken in the social and historical context of their lives and thus in relation to the history of the people.

In the Old Testament, a fully elaborated theology of election was first offered by Deuteronomy, and its concept of election became basic to all subsequent developments. A summary of this concept is given in the form of Moses' words to the people: "For you are a people holy to the LORD your God; the LORD your God has chosen you to be a people for his own possession, out of all the peoples that are on the face of the earth. It was not because you were more in number than any other people that the LORD set his love upon you and chose you, for you were the fewest of all peoples; but it is because the LORD loves you, and is keeping the oath which he swore to your fathers, that the LORD has brought you out with a mighty hand, and redeemed you from the house of bondage, from the hand of

Pharaoh king of Egypt" (Deut. 7:6–8).

What is interpreted here as being chosen, or elected, is the event of Israel's rescue from Egyptian oppression and especially from the pursuing army of the Pharaoh at the Sea of Weeds. This historical event is seen as an expression of God's love for Israel, and this love is further interpreted as God's preference for Israel over all other nations. Election is understood as a selection of one out of many. It is the goal of such selection that the beloved one is to belong to God and to share community with God. The historical event of the exodus is understood as providing the foundation of a continuing community, i.e., of God's history with Israel on the basis of his covenant.

The section from Deuteronomy includes, however, a hint of even earlier events in speaking of an oath of God sworn to the fathers. This phrase is but faintly reminiscent of the fact that there had been earlier ideas of election connected with the fathers, especially with Jacob, but also with Abraham. Deuteronomy had to play down these traditions by speaking only of an "oath" of God instead of election, because it wanted to reserve that term for the exodus event. This interesting detail shows that the idea of election implied singularity, while there were in fact several, competing traditions that reported elective events. Consequently, in the process of transmission it became a debated issue just which historical event was to be recognized as providing the foundation for all the subsequent history of God with Israel. That unique dignity was claimed by representing it as the event of God's election of Israel.

The tradition that traces God's election back to the fathers includes another important variation, especially in the case of Abraham (Ps. 105:6ff., 42ff.). From the Genesis report on Abraham's calling, it could be remembered that the goal of God's election was not simply Abraham and his posterity as object of God's love. God's goal transcends Abraham and his posterity, since the promise of God's blessing is extended through Abraham to "all the families of the earth" (Gen. 12:3). Thus the identification of Abraham's vocation as constituting God's election of his posterity introduces a universalistic tendency into the notion of election (cf. Sirach 44:19ff.). While in Deuteronomy (and in the case of Jacob) God's election is restricted to Israel, this particularism is placed within a more comprehensive context by the Abraham tradition. The tension between a particularistic and a more universalistic interpretation of God's election of Israel has been effective from this point on through Jewish history. In the light of the New Testament this ambiguity is clarified in favor of a more universalistic intention. The particularism of the love of God for the elected one is to be related to the more comprehensive horizon of God's love for all mankind. The chosen one, then, is assigned a function for that wider context. He is elected in order to serve as God's agent in relation to a more comprehensive object of God's love. Therefore the chosen one belongs to God precisely in serving God's greater purpose in the world. This conception is exemplified by the combination in Psalm 78 of the election of David and of Zion, which had been a special tradition legitimating the dynasty of David, with God's election of Israel. God "chose David his servant, and took him from the sheepfolds . . . to be the shepherd of Jacob his people, of Israel his inheritance" (Ps. 78:70–71). In a similar way, Second Isaiah spoke of the people of Israel as chosen to act as God's servant among the nations to the effect that "he will bring forth justice to the nations" (Isa. 42:1).

The elected one is accountable to God for the performance of his mission. Concerning Israel as a people, this applies specifically to the observance of the law, since the function of Israel among the nations is to witness to God's will to justice among men. In this way, Isaiah already envisioned a pilgrimage of all the nations to Zion in order to be instructed by the God of Jacob, " 'that he may teach us his ways and that we may walk in his paths.' For out of Zion shall go forth the law, and the word of the LORD from Jerusalem" (Isa. 2:3). Here the covenant of God with Israel is given a significance for all mankind. It is in the same line that Second Isaiah identifies the mission of Israel as bringing forth justice to the nations (ch. 42:1). The difference between Second Isaiah and Proto-Isaiah suggested by the historical experience of Jerusalem's fall to Nebuchadnezzar and of the Babylonian exile and the following dispersion of the people is only this: the nations are no longer expected to flock to Jerusalem, but Israel is turning to the nations in order to enlighten them by justice.

It would be easy to extend this line from Second Isaiah to early Christianity, especially to the early Christian interpretation of Jesus' mission and of its significance for all mankind. This interpretation draws heavily from Second Isaiah and from his concept of the servant of God. But for the present purpose of elucidating the structure of the concept of election, it is even more important to consider a further structural element characteristic of the historical concept of election in contrast to the classical doctrine.

The accountability of the elected one for his mission in the context of God's further purpose in history entails the possibility of his failure and consequently of his rejection or reprobation. In the classical doctrine of election there is no room for successive acts such as electing someone first and rejecting him later on. Why is such a sequence of acts excluded in that doctrine? Because election is conceived of as an eternal rather than a historical act. Moreover, the chosen one is not understood to be elected for some function within the wider context of God's design, but the purpose of his election is only for his own final salvation. Therefore there is nothing that he could be held accountable for so that the chosen one could be rejected again.

In the historical concept of election, however, as documented in the Old Testament, the chosen one is certainly destined to salvation, but not unconditionally so. His personal salvation is connected with his mission of serving the more universal purpose of God. Therefore, if he fails to live up to his mission, he becomes a candidate for rejection or reprobation, although his election was certainly meant to be definitive. The close relationship between election and accountability was emphasized in the prophetic tradition as early as Amos. While he starts with a comforting reminder of the people's chosenness, he continues his argument with an unexpected turn. He derives from that chosenness, not a guarantee of Israel's security, but rather a proclamation of impending judgment: "You only have I known of all the families of the earth; therefore I will punish you for all your iniquities" (Amos 3:2). Psalm 78 stated that after the Assyrian destruction of the Northern Kingdom God "utterly rejected Israel. He forsook his dwelling at Shiloh, the tent where he dwelt among men" (Ps. 78:59–60). Little more than a century after that event, Jeremiah proclaimed a word of God announcing that he would do the same to the Kingdom of Judah: "I will do to the house which is called by my name, and in which you trust, and to the place which I gave to you and to your fathers, as I did to Shiloh" (Jer. 7:14; cf. v. 29).

But reprobation need not be more final than election. The same Jeremiah called to God: "Hast thou utterly rejected Judah? . . . Do not spurn us, for thy name's sake; do not dishonor thy glorious throne; remember and do not break thy covenant with us" (Jer. 14:19, 21). It was only after the catastrophe of Jerusalem, however, that Jeremiah received word from God that he would indeed hold on to his covenant (Jer. 33:20ff.). Now the prophet Ezekiel announced that God for the sake of his holy name would return the exiles to their native land (Ezek. 36:22ff.). Both Jeremiah and Ezekiel announced a new covenant to be offered to the people. A late addition to The Book of Isaiah even speaks explicitly of a repetition of the first election, a rather paradoxical notion in the light of the uniqueness implicit in that term: "The Lord will have compassion on Jacob and will again choose Israel, and will set them in their own land" (Isa. 14:1).

The historical concept of election, then, in contrast to what has been called the abstract notion of election, refers to a historical event as constitutive for being chosen. And it assigns a mission to the elected one that relates him to a more comprehensive context of God's design in history. Thus the chosen individual is related to the people and the people to mankind in a similar way. At the same time, the interrelation of election and mission entails the consequence that the elected one is accountable to God for his mission to the world and may be rejected again in case of his failure. Yet the act of election is meant to be definitive. Even in the case of failure there is still a chance in calling upon the faithfulness, self-identity, and perseverance of God.

Notwithstanding the predominance of this historical concept of election in the Old Testament, the roots of the abstract form of the notion are discovered to be as early as the postexilic period of Jewish thought. From that time on, the election of the people was interpreted restrictively as being meant for the righteous ones only. Thus the entire Book of Enoch is addressed to those righteous and elected ones who will be alive on the day of judgment when all the ungodly and sinful people will be done away with (Enoch 1:1). Together with this concentration on the election of individuals blessed for their own sake, another change occurs: the historicity of the elective act of God fades. In the Book of Enoch it is still the election of Abraham that contains the election of all the righteous individuals of later generations (Enoch 93:5). But the historical act of God's election of Abraham and of his family was now changed into a statement of God's prescience, or foreknowledge, concerning those members of later generations who will turn out to be righteous.

This emphasis on the prescience of God renders it plausible that later on the moment of election was removed from history altogether into God's eternal foreknowledge of those individuals who shall present themselves as living in accordance with his eternal law. History is no longer the field of God's elective action. Not even the revelation of what was decided upon in God's eternal foreknowledge is understood henceforth to occur in history. Although the law has been revealed as a criterion of who belongs to the number of the chosen, their identity will be definitively disclosed only in the act of eschatological judgment. In this way, in the Book of Enoch, the Son of Man is said to have been chosen by God before the creation of the world, and all the other elected ones together with him (Enoch 62:7ff.; 39:4f.). The "selection" among the deeds of men to be performed by the Son of Man in the act of eschatological judgment (ch. 45:3) will correspond to God's eternal foreknowledge. Thus the course of history between its primordial beginning and its eschatological end no longer has any constitutive significance for the issue of election.

The salient point that explains most of the changes in this concept as compared to the Old Testament idea of God's elective activity in history is its individualism. If the act of election is no longer directed to the people at large, but only to those individuals who will present themselves as righteous, then the whole subject inevitably becomes a matter of God's foreknowledge of those righteous individuals whose righteousness is measured by the law that expresses his eternal will. Beyond that, there remains only the question for the final revelation of who belongs to the number of the chosen and will therefore enter the eschatological community of those who truly performed the will of God.

How did this change to individualism in the idea of election come to pass? In order to understand this transition, one has to turn back once more to the situation of the exile after the Babylonians had conquered Jerusalem. In The Book of Jeremiah as well as The Book of Ezekiel there are indications that the righteousness of God himself was called into question at that time. Why did God allow this disaster to come upon a generation that after the promulgation of Deuteronomy at the time of the pious king Josiah had been so eager to live according to the provisions of the law? If former generations had not done so, why had they not been punished, but this one instead? Both prophets report a sarcastic saying that actually presents a distillate of that mood: "The fathers have eaten sour grapes, and the children's teeth are set on edge." In such an unnatural way, according to this epigram, God had been dealing with this people. Both prophets took this as a serious objection against the righteousness of God. Jeremiah promised that in the coming days of the new covenant it would be otherwise (Jer. 31:30).

Ezekiel went even further in proclaiming that from his time on a new regulation was to be effective: "The soul that sins shall die. The son shall not suffer for the iniquity of the father, nor the father suffer for the iniquity of the son; the righteousness of the righteous shall be upon himself, and the wickedness of the wicked shall be upon himself" (Ezek. 18:20).[1]

This new concentration on the individual in Jewish thought since the time of the exile has had far-reaching consequences. It led to the development of the expectation of a future life beyond death for the individual, in order to provide adequate compensation for human actions, be they good or bad.[2] Within this life span, such compensation does not always occur to the individual as it should according to the justice of God. Therefore there must be a future for the individual beyond death so that he or she may receive the appropriate recompense corresponding to the individual actions of each during this life.

Similarly, important consequences seem to have followed from the new individualism concerning the understanding of election and God's action in history. Since God's righteousness was now to become manifest in the individual, the individual must become the actual aim of his elective love. In choosing a people, God was now understood as actually having chosen individuals. The idea of the prophets that only a remnant of the people would finally enjoy the salvation intended by its election had already prepared such a concentration of God's election on the individuals who would hold on to his covenant. But if now the individuals were made the point of reference of God's action, his election had to become a matter of his foreknowledge concerning the future righteousness of some individuals in distinction from others. Thus the rising individualism of the period after the Babylonian exile explains how the abstract concept of election originated. Later on, this was elaborated into the Christian doctrine of election.

The emergence of this view, to be sure, is not only due to the inherent logic of the individual as the place to manifest God's justice. Very rarely are historical processes sufficiently motivated by the intrinsic logic of fundamental ideas. In most cases they need additional incentives to focus the intention of people upon the implications of such principles. In the present case such additional incentive was presumably contributed by the historical experience of the Jewish people after the return of the exiles from Babylon. Palestine continued to be dominated by foreign powers. God apparently withdrew from the actualities of the political history of his people. The new experience of God's absence from history, however, called for a compensating rationale. That was offered by the idea that God had determined from eternity the sequence of epochs and events that was to be revealed in the end.[3] This assumption had, no doubt, a stabilizing effect for individuals and their religious community as they were living under adverse circumstances. And this also continued to be the positive function of the abstractly individualistic concept of election later on in Christian history. It stabilized the confidence of the individual and of communities built of such individuals over against a strange and repellent world. It corresponds to the mentality of those who conceive of themselves as having emigrated from history. It can also serve, if joined by additional motifs, as a powerful starting point for reconquering the world of historical experience.

In early Christianity the postexilic concept of election as an eternal decision of God (hidden in the present world) concerning the final salvation of a certain number of individuals continued to be influential. Most importantly, it occurs in a sentence attributed to Jesus: "Many are called, but few are chosen" (Matt. 22:14). Here, in a characteristic form, to be chosen is set in contrast to being called. To be called is a historical event, while the identity of the elected one is hidden in this world and not to be revealed before the end. This sentence only echoes the understanding of election that was prevailing in postexilic Jewish thought. Similarly, the Gospel of John uses the idea of a limited number of elected individuals, chosen from eternity. But Jews combined that idea with the mission of the Son in the world, the goal of which is to collect and redeem the elected ones. The individualistic concept of election occurs also in Paul, especially in his reflections in Rom. 9:6ff. on the children of promise as representing the true children of Abraham, which is documented among other arguments by Mal. 1:2–3: "I have loved Jacob but I have hated Esau." In his tendency to keep the election of God independent from the behavior of the chosen ones, Paul turns his argument against the traditional understanding of God's election as conditioned by his foreknowledge of the behavior of his creatures. Nevertheless he argues on the basis of the assumption that election is an eternal act of God related directly to certain individuals concerning their salvation.

There is also a different line of argument in early Christian tradition, a fresh start for a historical conception of election. That development began with Jesus' choosing of the twelve disciples, an act that is presented by Luke (ch. 6:13; cf. Acts 1:2) and John (chs. 6:70; 13:18; 15:16) explicitly in terms of an election. After his resurrection the elective activity of Christ was extended to all those who accept the apostolic gospel. Thus Paul calls the faithful "the chosen ones of God" (Rom. 8:33) and refers to individual Christians as "elected in the Lord" (Rom. 16:13). Here, the idea of election is clearly connected with the missionary activity of early Christianity. Acts (ch. 15:7) and the letter to the Ephesians legitimate this missionary expansion of the Christian church by tracing it back to a primordial decision of God. He has chosen us in Christ "before the foundation of the world" (Eph. 1:4). The same reversal occurs in the Gospel of John: the reference to eternity no longer indicates a withdrawal from historical time, but emphasizes the eternal importance of what happens in time.

In consequence of his extending God's election to all those who faithfully accept the apostolic gospel, Paul also includes the Christian church in the old concept of the people of God. In Rom., ch. 11, Paul presents the question whether, in view of Israel's rejection of the gospel, God "rejected his people" (v.1). His answer is emphatically negative. How could Christians trust in their comparatively recent status of being elected if God did not faithfully hold fast to his election of Israel? Paul finds it possible to reconcile this experience of only sporadic acceptance of the gospel by Jews to his belief in the irrevocableness of God's election by appealing to the idea of a chosen remnant as mentioned in the story of Elijah. He obviously applies the notion of the chosen remnant to the Christians who, like himself (v. 1), came from the Jews.[4] Yet he did not abandon the majority of the Jewish people to their fate in the imminent judgment. Rather, he affirms that "a hardening has come upon part of Israel, until the full number of the Gentiles come in, and so all Israel will be saved" (vs. 25–26).

Thus Paul retains the concept of Israel as the chosen people of God in spite of Israel's rejection of the gospel. He even finds a redemptive meaning in that disturbing experience: "Through their trespass salvation has come to the Gentiles, so as to make Israel jealous" (v. 11). Paul obviously expected that the paradigmatic righteousness of the Gentile Christians would induce Israel to recognize their behavior as a sign of election and therefore to join them. Unfortunately, this has not been the character of Jewish-Christian relations throughout history.

In a more clear-cut way than Paul, Peter addresses the Christians as the chosen people of God: "Once you were no people but now you are God's people" (I Peter 2:10). In distinction from Paul, there was no further mention of the Jews except by reference to those who stumbled at the cornerstone that God laid down in Zion (I Peter 1:8). After the year 70, the destruction of the Jerusalem Temple by Titus was taken as a visible sign of God's judgment passed on the Jews. The Christians—more and more identified with the Gentile Christians—felt themselves free to claim the title of God's people exclusively for themselves. This tendency culminated in the letter of Barnabas, which not only replaced the old people of God by the new people, but even denied the Jews any claim to having been the people of God at one time. Since the Jews did not accept the covenant offered to them by Moses, as Barnabas thinks evident from their building themselves a golden image, they have never been God's people (Barn. 14.1ff.). Hence it was reserved to the Christians first to become God's people to whom the promises of the Old Testament relate. Less unfair to the Jews was Melito of Sardis in conceding to them at least the dignity of having foreshadowed the glory of the church: "The people was valuable, before the church emerged, and the law was admirable before the Gospel rose to light. But since the church was established and the Gospel was proclaimed, the model got devalued and transmitted its power to the truth" (Hom. §41f.).

The same contrast between a provisional model and the full reality exhibited by the church was developed by other theologians of the second and third centuries. Hippolytus of Rome distinguished the church as the new people of God from the old people which had defected from its vocation.[5] This account, fashioned in a more historical form, became the predominant concept in dealing with the relation of Christianity to Judaism. The exclusivism of a consciousness of eschatological fulfillment on the part of the church was similar in all these examples. Precisely that exclusivism, which is either paradoxical or frightening in combination with Christian universalism, constitutes the problem in the development of Christian relations to Israel. These Christian voices from the second century were a far cry from Paul's effort to preserve as irrevocable the claim of the Jewish people to being the people of God. Paul clung to his conviction even though at his time the actual borderline of the chosen people had shrunk to a remnant, while at the same time it was extended to include the Gentiles. This conception of Paul's, to be sure, could perhaps not remain completely unchanged after the Gentile Christians had become the overwhelming majority in Christianity. But still Paul's warning could have prevented the Gentile Christians from cutting off themselves from the tree into which they had been implanted. Instead, the Gentile Christian church did just that. Certainly the church of that period decided against Marcion by retaining the Jewish Bible as an authoritative document of the God to whom the church of Christ confessed. But the continuity with Israel that came to expression in that decision remained ambiguous, since it amounted to denying the Jewish people its claim to the document of its own religious heritage.

It was in its relationship to Judaism that the church had to decide for the first time on either accepting an element of pluralism in its understanding of God's history with mankind and of its own place in that history, or embracing a concept of its chosenness to the exclusion of everybody else. The decision fell in favor of the second alternative. The subsequent history of Christianity has demonstrated the dangerous consequences of dogmatism and of an extended series of incessant separations and divisions issuing from that dogmatic exclusivism. It is important to realize that the underlying fault of this painful process came first to the fore in the church's relationship to the Jewish people. It has remained present throughout Christian history. The inherent danger of exclusivism could have been anticipated on the basis of what the prophets of the Old Testament tell about the pride of the chosen one that hardens his heart and leads to his disaster. Perhaps the abstract individualism of the classical doctrine of election that no longer dealt with a possible rejection of the chosen one contributed to Christian carelessness about this danger.

The issue of the "people of God" represents in Christian tradition the continuous presence of a concretely historical concept of election different from the individualistic scope of the classical doctrine. It belongs to the greatness of Augustine's work on the City of God that he managed once more to combine the two traditions. He did so, however, on the basis of the notion of God's eternal decision in favor of some individuals rather than others. This method deeply affected Augustine's vision of the church, and by his overwhelming authority this perspective became extremely influential. The chosen individuals constitute the community of the chosen ones which Augustine called the City of God over against the secular city, the state. Of course, there have always been some chosen individuals throughout the course of human history. Consequently there has always existed some form of the city of God, since Abel the son of Adam, over against the terrestrial city that seeks the terrestrial peace through war and political struggle and domination. Although that City of God according to Augustine is primarily a spiritual reality, an invisible community of the chosen dispersed among all nations, it also existed at one time as the people of Israel and exists at present in the form of the Christian church. Thus, an element of historical sequence and the "spiritual" idea of an invisible community of the chosen are combined in Augustine's thought. But this idea of an invisible church, based upon the individualistic and dualistic nature of his concept of election, became predominant in the repercussions of Augustine's thought throughout the Middle Ages and still in Luther's concept of the two kingdoms. The other element, the issue of the people of God and the question of its continuity from Israel to the Christian church, disappeared from the post-Augustinian doctrine of election. It became less important even in the concept of the church except as a typological or allegorical ornament.[6] Its fading in the medieval church corresponded to the lack of a continuing need to define itself in relation to Israel. At the same time the church no longer understood itself in terms of corporate election, but rather as the instrument of the kingly rule of Christ. However, the historical and social question for the people of God as representing the issue of chosenness in the process of Christian history did not disappear altogether. It went underground, as it were, and exerted a formative influence in the political history of the West.

It is an important event in our time that the concept of the people of God as related to the doctrine of the church has been rediscovered. This happened at about the same time in different places and traditions. In discussions within the World Council of Churches the term "people of God" recommended itself as one of those Biblical phrases which have not been seized upon by confessionally disputed dogmatics. Thus it had not been identified with a particular denominational perspective. The term could refer to all of Christianity in distinction from the plurality of churches.[7] At the same time, the phrase was rediscovered in Roman Catholic theology and finally given an important place by the Second Vatican Council in its constitution on the church.[8] Here it was appreciated as offering a more general and unrestricted basis for the doctrine of the church than a description of its nature in hierarchical or juridical or even sacramental terms could provide. But the World Council of Churches as well as the Roman Catholic Church used the phrase "people of God," as if it were self-evident, as a designation of Christianity or even of the church.[9] The difficult problems that arise in using that concept today concerning the relationship of Christianity to the Jewish people, and also concerning the difference between a people of God and the church as an institution, have not yet fully been realized. This, however, indicates also the potential of that concept. Laying claim to it requires a redefinition of the church in terms of a theology of history and of a historical theory of election.

4

The Christian Empire
and Civil Religion in Christianity

IT HAS BECOME CUSTOMARY IN MODERN THEOLOGICAL LITERA-
ture to deplore the Constantinian epoch. It is considered a
downfall of Christianity from the moral prominence of the
martyrs' church into corruption by collaboration and even
identification with the political power of the Empire. There are
data which seem to justify such a judgment. Most Christian
bishops and theologians did welcome the use of violence, sanc-
tioned by the political authorities, against the cultic life and
temples of other religions. They did not protest the persecution
of their adherents and the enforcement of Christianization.
They were prepared to support and legitimate the imperial
authority and its actions in almost every case. They accepted
more or less incisive interference of the imperial power with
the responsibilities of the church. Concerning all these points,
especially the last one, there also occurred remarkable excep-
tions, examples of resistance and courage. But the general
situation corresponds largely to the critical description.

The most serious charge is that of intolerance, and we have
to come back to that subject later. It would be unfair, however,
to pass judgment on so complex a historical phenomenon as the
Constantinian epoch only on the basis of this particular aspect.
Before dismissing such a phenomenon, one should appreciate
the paradigmatic significance and continuous impact of the
contribution of that epoch to the issue of Christianity and
politics. In a consideration of this contribution, the most im-

portant point is not the Christian legitimation of a monarchical form of government because of its alleged correspondence to God's monarchical rule over the cosmos. Prior to all questions concerning the specific form of political government is a clarification of the underlying rationale of the Byzantine concept of a symphony, a harmonious connection and solidarity of church and empire. The issue is not the general question of the coexistence of the church with political government, but specifically its relation to the Empire.

In order to appreciate the distinctive significance of this issue for the ancient church, it may be helpful for us to turn to a remark of Eusebius', the man who developed the theological legitimation of the Christian empire. In his history of the church, before he begins to report on the course of events constituting the ecclesiastical history, Eusebius offers reflections with which a modern church historian would hardly begin. He wants to prevent any suspicion that he would deal just with recent developments. Rather, he does his best to suggest to his readers that the history beginning with Jesus Christ was prepared long ago. Indeed, it originated from God at creation. And together with Jesus Christ there emerged— as it was predetermined—"a new people, neither small nor weak nor dwelling somewhere in a corner of the earth, but the most numerous and pious of all peoples, indestructible and invincible because it lives under the protection of God forever."[10] Eusebius argues that this people, although admittedly it arose only recently, continues the heritage, as Jesus Christ himself did, of "God's friends of old," the patriarchs and prophets of Israel, so that its religion is actually the very oldest and true one.

For the purpose of the present argument it is important that the emergence of that new people sets the stage for Eusebius' subsequent presentation of the history of the church. Thus, the church, the history of which Eusebius describes, is not only a religious institution beside other institutions in society. It is a new *people* taking shape in the course of that history, which happens according to God's design that had been determined

long ago. Thus the rise of that people to prominence was
inevitable. Consequently, all attempts to suppress its emergence and expansion were doomed to failure from the outset.
Since the issue was a people, however, and not just a particular
institution, its final victory had to take place in the form of
political emancipation. Thus, toward the end of his church
history Eusebius refers to Constantine and Licinius, who, according to him, had been aroused and inspired by God against
the ungodly tyrants responsible for the previous persecutions
(*Hist. eccl.* IX. 9. 1). Remarkably enough, however, Eusebius
was not completely satisfied with concluding his presentation
of the history of the church with Constantine's victory over
Maxentius in 312 which "cleaned the world of the hostility
against God" (IX. 11). Nor did he stop with including the
Milan edict of toleration of 313 (X. 5). He continued his report
through repeated additions to the restoration of the unity of
the Roman Empire by Constantine's triumph over Licinius in
324 (X. 9. 6). Why could he regard that event as the finally
adequate conclusion of a history of the early church? In the last
books of his work, Eusebius does not argue by reference to the
political implications of his earlier description of the Christians
as a people, although he continues to speak of the Christian
people (*laos*, X. 4. 65) as Constantine himself had done (X. 6).
Still his report on the history of the church concludes with the
restoration of the Roman Empire on the basis of the true
religion. This suggests some intrinsic correspondence between
the nature of his peculiar subject and that political event.
Actually Eusebius explicitly expounded the correspondence between the Christian faith and the Roman Empire elsewhere
and in doing so he followed a theological tradition that can be
traced back to the New Testament itself.

   The predominant view in early Christianity concerning the
relationship between church and Empire was that of a fundamental opposition between the two, since the Empire per-
secuted those who confessed to the only true God. There is
clear evidence of opposition between church and Empire in
the book of Revelation and later on. Especially under the

impact of apocalyptic thought, Rome was seen as representing
the last and worst ungodly power in the sequence of empires
foretold by the vision of Daniel. In the beginning of the third
century, after the great persecution under Septimius Severus,
this view was represented by Hippolytus of Rome. In his *Commentary on Daniel* he referred to the coincidence of the origins
of the Roman Empire at Augustus' time with the birth of
Christ and he did so in terms of a "Satanic imitation" of the
Kingdom of God, the heavenly emperor, by the kingdom of
this world.[11] The imitation consisted in the Augustan peace,
the celebrated achievement of the pacification of the Mediterranean world by the Roman Empire. Hippolytus, however,
insisted that this peace exhibited only a falsifying image of the
heavenly peace of the Kingdom of God that was introduced
into this world by Christ.

The coincidence of the birth of Christ with the rise of
Augustus was a common point of reference in early Christian
literature. The first to find it worthy of mention was Luke in
his Gospel (Luke 2:1), although there was no further indication
as to the significance of the correspondence of the two events.
Luke did not intend such a negative and antithetic qualification of the Roman Empire as Hippolytus did. In accordance
with his rather sympathetic attitude toward the Romans—as
it is documented in his tendency to play down the involvement
of Pilate in the proceedings against Jesus—Luke may rather
have implied that there existed some positive correspondence
between the birth of Christ and the rise of the Empire. In this
sense his observation was reiterated in Christian apologetic
literature during the second century.

In the third century, Origen offered a more profound interpretation of the issue. In his controversy with Celsus he wanted
to defend the Christian faith against the charge that it would
ruin the foundations of the Empire since it undercut the national religious traditions that had been treated with respect by
the Romans in order to secure the peace of the Empire. In
answering this charge, Origen points to the correspondence
between the universal peace brought to mankind by Christ and

the Augustan peace achieved by Roman unification and pacification of the ancient world at that time. With reference to
these events Origen registers the fulfillment of Ps. 72:7 in the
days of Christ, "because 'in his days righteousness came to
flourish and peace was achieved,' beginning at his birth. God
prepared the peoples for his teaching by causing their unification under the rule of the Roman emperor. There should not
be many kingdoms, because the nations would have continued
to regard one another as strangers, and thus the performance
of Jesus' commission to the apostles: 'Go and teach all nations'
would have been more difficult." Origen adds that without the
Roman Empire the nations would have continued to wage war
against one another, so that the peaceful doctrine of Jesus and
his veto against revenge could hardly have prevailed.[12]

In this as in other matters Eusebius followed his teacher
Origen,[13] but he applied his views to a changing situation. He
celebrated Constantine first for his restoration of the Augustan
Empire. Later on he proclaimed Constantine's rule as that of
the friend and vicegerent of the divine Logos ruling the world.
Constantine now appears as representing the heavenly rule of
Christ himself on earth.[14] Thus it is plausible that he is called
the common bishop of all, especially in his competence for
calling the bishops to synods and to an ecumenical council and
thus securing the unity of faith as the basis of the unity of the
Empire. In Eusebius' thought the imperial power becomes
increasingly an office of the universal church. One can do
justice to this position only if one remembers that the church
was not understood as a particularly religious institution, but
in terms of the people itself that is to be organized and guided
by bishops and emperor. This represents an element of continuity in the development of Eusebius' thought. The new and
central role of the Christians in the Empire under Constantine
caused Eusebius to change his original conception of Christianity as a new nation among other nations in order to attribute
to Christianity an even more universal function. Yet it is still
the same basic intention, as in the early chapters of his church
history, when he praised the singular importance of that recently emerging people.

The political theology of Eusebius expresses a complete unity of church and society. Its problem is that the distinction between the present situation of Christianity and the eschatological future of the Kingdom of God was replaced by another distinction: the Platonic one between the spiritual archetype of God's heavenly rule and its image in this life in the rule of the emperor. In consequence of this change the provisional character of any organization of social life—provisional even concerning alternative historical developments—over against the ultimate future of the Kingdom of God was lost sight of. Accordingly, the distinction between the function of the church on the one hand in securing for individuals access to their eternal salvation, and the provisional task of the political order of society on the other, was blurred. Later in Byzantine history, this distinction became an issue again, and only then the distinction between two offices—the office of the emperor and that of the bishops—within a society formed on the basis of the Christian faith was developed. Even then, however, Byzantine thought remained tempted to overestimate the finality of the temporal rule of the emperor, since he was believed to represent in this temporal world the invincible Kingdom of Christ himself.

That concept suffered a serious blow in 410 when the West Goths under Alaric conquered Rome, and Augustine had to defend the Christian faith against the charge of being responsible for the downfall of the Empire. Was the new God of the Christians unable or unwilling to take care of the well-being of the Empire as the traditional gods of Rome had done for so long? His answer, given in his work on the City of God,[15] was basically that the Kingdom of God is neither identical nor intrinsically connected with any form of political government on earth. The Christian faith, therefore, is no warrant for the enduring persistence of any form of political order. Christians make use of the temporal peace obtained by political order. Christians also contribute to the stability of such peace. Yet political peace will always be limited because of the ongoing contest for power and glory among individuals, groups, and nations. For this consequence of human sinfulness, the Christians cannot be blamed. Much less so can their God who has been offended by that sinfulness and whose judgment becomes manifest in the fate of kingdoms and empires.

The realism of Augustine's analysis of political processes must have been most impressive. But that realism was only an instrument serving Augustine's more peculiar purpose. It helped him achieve what he finally intended: the disengagement of Christianity from the fate of the Roman Empire. But in terms of political theory he paid a considerable price for what he got. That price is the dualism inherent in Augustine's perspective, the dualistic vision of a parallel development of the two kingdoms or cities throughout history. It is a perspective based upon his abstractly individualistic doctrine of double predestination constituting two different groups of people and thus providing the basis for their parallel developments through history. To Augustine himself, the former Manichee, that dualism may not necessarily have appeared as a disadvantage. But the consequence was a retreat of the Christian faith from political commitment and, instead, a concentration on the church in contrast to all political structures of society. A calm detachment, more or less familiar to every Western Christian, regarding the political order even in a predominantly Christian society is part of the heritage of Augustine. The Kingdom of God is no longer manifest, even provisionally, in the realization of certain principles of political order that correspond to the Christian faith as, for example, in a universal organization of political peace.[16] The Kingdom of God is now said to be manifest only in the church. According to Augustine, the church is not only heir and successor of the chosen people of Israel. The church is said to be even at present the Kingdom of Christ, the Kingdom of Heaven (*"Ecclesia et nunc est regnum Christi, regnumque coelorum," De civ. Dei* XX. 9. 1).[17]

Certainly Augustine was aware of the difference between the present pilgrimage and the future glory of the church, when it will have been purged from all admixture of and struggle against evil and wickedness. Nevertheless he explicitly calls the church even in its present form the Kingdom of Christ, the

Kingdom of Heaven. The eschatological difference between the future of God and the present was certainly done more justice to in Augustine's theology of history than in Byzantine Platonism. But at the same time, Augustine played down that difference concerning the church in emphasizing the continuity between the present church as exhibiting already the Kingdom of Christ and the future completion of that Kingdom. In addition, Augustine attributed this quality to the church in the more restrictive sense of the word, taken as a particular institution over against the political order. The church was no longer just another name for the Christian people in all dimensions of their life, including the political. By its distinction from the political order, the church had become a partial institution over against other such institutions, even in a society of Christians. The Augustinian dualism thus cut into the life of every Christian, because every Christian had to participate in the political and economic order too, in addition to his membership in the church. On these terms to identify the church with the Kingdom of Christ turned out to be an ambiguous and rather dangerous position. On the one hand it deprived the organization of society in the context of the Christian tradition of its religious meaning. However, according to the insights of modern sociology—as it is represented for instance by Talcott Parsons' analysis of the social system—such a vacuum is not possible since religion is of basic importance for the unity of society. Therefore, a failure of Christian theology to provide a religious interpretation of the social system only leaves the scene to some other such interpretation. On the other hand, and especially because of that need for a religious legitimation of society, Augustine's identification of the church with the Kingdom of Christ entailed potentially all the claims of the medieval church over against the political order of the Christian people.[18]

Augustine was hardly aware of these consequences, because he envisioned the church as a spiritual reality, not as a politically powerful institution. But the church is also an institution within the social context. Moreover, the issue of a religious legitimation of the social system proved to be unavoidable. It is therefore not surprising that the medieval church, accustomed to identifying itself with the Kingdom of Christ, came to claim exclusive competence concerning the religious legitimation of medieval society. This trend became apparent in Augustine's own behavior, contrary to his theory, in his approval of the use of coercive political measures in dealing with the Donatists in North Africa. Thus, there obviously is a line that leads from his position to the clericalism of the medieval church. On the other hand, given Augustine's distinction between the church and the political organization of society, it is also understandable that a Christian interpretation of the political order of society was again developed in medieval society in distinction from the clerical authority of the church that had to be considered as only a partial institution within the whole body of the Christian people. Thus, in spite of Augustine's authority and in spite of the dominating position of the Roman Catholic Church in Western Christianity, a revival of Byzantine political ideas occurred in the early medieval period.[19] It was not only the glamorous memory of Imperial Rome, not only lust for power and pride in the glory of a native king, that induced people of the Carolingian epoch to look for a renewal of the Roman Empire in what formerly had been its Western part.[20] There was also awareness of the spiritual kinship of all Christians as one people, not only by common loyalty to the Roman Church but also in relation to the Byzantine empire. This is quite evident in the history of Charlemagne. Such an awareness did not exclude, of course, some element of competition with the Byzantine emperor for equal dignity. And yet, after he had accepted the imperial crown from Pope Leo III,[21] Charlemagne avoided the use of titles such as *Imperator Romanorum* that would get him into conflict with the claims of the Byzantine emperor. He was anxious to have his imperial position recognized and accepted by the Byzantine emperor even at the price of territorial concessions in Italy.[22] This endeavor was not dictated by political expedience, but rather by Charlemagne's appreciation of the kind of office entrusted to him. He understood his office as royal and sacerdotal at the same time, in succession of David, the chosen king of God's chosen people,[23] representing the rule of Christ himself over his people and thus acting as a substitute for Christ.[24] Most of these elements are also explicitly stated in the Frankish order of coronation dating from the ninth and tenth centuries. In the same way, later emperors used the title *vicarius Christi.*[25] When Innocent III in the thirteenth century arrogated that title to the papacy, there was clearly a political claim involved. Until then the pope had been understood to be the vicar of Peter, while the emperor was believed to act as the vicar of Christ, the heavenly king, on earth. The combination of royal and sacerdotal elements in the idea of the imperial office was in continuity with the Byzantine tradition. It meant, of course, latent conflict with the claims of the church in Western Christianity.

The renewal of the imperial idea in the West exemplifies the limitations of the Augustinian theory. It restricted the spiritual attributes of Christians as God's own people to the church as a particular institution in Christianity. The renaissance of a religious interpretation of society—be it in terms of a Christian empire or of Christian kingdoms, in each case combining sacerdotal and royal elements in the conception of political office—demonstrates that the religious issue in the society of Christians cannot be made an exclusive prerogative of the church which is only a particular institution in such a society. On the contrary, the significance of such an institution depends on the religious understanding of the entire social system. Insofar as the church as a separate institution, over against the political structure of society, embodies the eschatological character of the Christian faith, it is aware of the distinction between the ultimate and the provisional. Yet it is the entire social texture of human life, and especially its political system, that is given the promise of eschatological fulfillment in the advent of the Kingdom of God. The *people* is chosen, not a particular institution of the people, and as much as the institutional church reminds the people of its future homeland, the very existence

72 *Human Nature, Election, and History*

of the people exhibits an anticipation of that future in all the dimensions of its life. If the official doctrine of the church does not do justice to this complex situation by correlating church and political structure within a society constituted on the basis of the Christian heritage, if rather the religious issue is considered a prerogative of the institutional church to the exclusion of other institutions, then a *civil religion* develops in Christianity besides the official doctrine of the church. The roots of this development in Western Christianity go back to the early Middle Ages.

The term "civil religion" comes from the Stoic tripartition of mythical, civil, and natural religion. It stands in distinction from the mythical religion of the poets inventing all sorts of stories about the mutual relationships and involvements of gods. It is distinguished, too, from the natural religion of philosophers searching for the true nature of divine reality. Civil religion represents that form of religion which is sustained by the political authorities for the purpose of legitimating the political system and securing its well-being. In Greek and Roman history, civil or political religion constituted a peculiar type and not just a common function of religion, because the poets had no authority. In Israel, however, the political aspect was integrated in the common process of the religious tradition, although not always without difficulties. The prophetic tradition represented the religious authority over against the kings. Hence there was no room left for a civil religion as an independent factor. This was precisely because the political issue, the place of the king and messianic hope, was made an element of the common religious tradition itself, subordinate to the theocratic claim.

In the case of Christianity, there was also a strong theocratic tendency in proclaiming the Kingdom of Christ in contrast to the authority of the Roman emperor. Theoretically, this theocratic tendency triumphed when the Roman emperor subordinated himself to the rule of Christ. Practically, of course, precautions had to be taken to secure that such a subordination was more than self-legitimating lip service. To some degree the possibility of checking the pretended subordination of the emperor to the Kingdom of Christ was provided in Byzantium by insistence upon the independent authority of the bishops in spiritual matters and especially on their competence to judge the orthodoxy of the emperor himself. This independent authority and competence of the bishops constituted the most important difference from the pre-Christian political religion of the Empire, since neither the poets nor the priests had enjoyed such independent authority. If the absence of such an authority to which the political order would be accountable is characteristic of political or civil religion as a special type of religion, then the Christian empire of Byzantium was not an example of civil religion. Rather, it was theocratic, provided one does not mistake theocracy for a reign of priests, which is only a perversion of it.

On the basis of Augustine's spiritualistic and ecclesiocentric interpretation of the rule of Christ and the people of God, however, a vacuum, in terms of religious interpretation, became apparent in the political realm. This vacuum was filled by the continuation and renewal of the idea of the Christian empire and by a religious interpretation of the function and dignity of kings and emperors in continuity with King David. It was only in Western Christianity that these political ideas, because of their contrast to the official Augustinian doctrine, obtained a status of something like a Christian civil religion, which otherwise should be regarded as a contradiction in terms, given the theocratic tendency of the Christian faith. This peculiar and complex situation helps to explain the clashes between the church and the political authorities that occurred in Western Christianity during the course of the Middle Ages.

The issue of a civil religion arose in Western Christianity not only in the form of the imperial idea and the renewal of the Western Empire on the basis of the new Germanic and Romanic kingdoms. Closely connected with it, a special brand of nationalism emerged and finally spread all over Europe. The origins of modern nationalism are usually dated from the French Revolution, and there is certainly some point in this account if the sovereignty of the people is understood to be basic for the idea of nationalism. But it is possible and more adequate to interpret this modern phenomenon in the framework of a more comprehensive historical context. It is generally acknowledged that the French Revolution owed much to the ideas of the British civil war of the seventeenth century. The religious idea of a peculiar national calling that culminated in England during the Cromwellian period can be traced back to the rivalry between France and Germany that developed after the end of the Carolingian period. It will be argued that this sense of chosenness which is characteristic of civil religion in Christianity belongs to the very heart of nationalism as it developed in the history of Western Christianity.

The rivalry between what were later called France and Germany began in the ninth century when a dispute between the different parts of the Frankish empire developed over the heritage of Charlemagne.[26] Charles the Bald ran in competition with his German brothers both for the largest part of the territory and for the imperial crown of his grandfather. Shortly before his death he was indeed crowned emperor by Pope John VIII in 875. After that time the kings of France claimed again and again for their own nation and kingdom the authentic succession of the empire of Charlemagne in opposition to the German emperors of the Middle Ages whom they considered usurpators. The situation could have been less confused, perhaps, if the renewal of the Western Empire by Charlemagne had been achieved in closer cooperation with the Byzantine emperor instead of being precipitated by the initiative of a pope concerned for the political stabilization of his own authority and jurisdiction in the West. In fact, however, the separation of Western Christianity from the East, to which the coronation of Charlemagne certainly contributed, was quickly followed by the rupture in Western Christianity itself because of the quarrel between the Germans and the French over the heritage of Charlemagne.

The French claim to the authentic succession of Charlemagne's empire over all of Western Christianity was not only vigorous in the proud spirit of French medieval knights, as it was celebrated by French historians of the first crusade. The same national pride was also called upon by the popes in their contest against the German emperors. In return, in 1202 Pope Innocent III told the king of France to recognize no superior in temporal matters, and twelve years later he called him the most Christian king, *rex christianissimus.* [27] From this time on, the ideological position of the king profited immensely from the skill and learning of French lawyers who were eager to point out all the implications of such titles and acknowledgments. In the beginning of the fourteenth century one of them, Pierre Dubois, argued that Christ had elected the French king—successor of Moses and David—to higher honor than other lords and kings in Christendom because the Christian faith, as the pope himself had asserted, found a more reliable basis in France than anywhere else. As Pierre Dubois explicitly said, the French people in a special way is chosen by God *(in peculiarem populum electum a Domino).* [28] Therefore the king of France is the most appropriate prince in Christianity to preside over "the entire republic of all Christians" *(tota respublica omnium Christicolarum),* particularly because of his descendance from Charlemagne and consequently because of his legal claim to the imperial office and dignity. All these ideas were *en vogue* two centuries before the appearance of Joan of Arc gave to the French national sentiment that tremendous boost which some authors consider the birth of French nationalism. It has been shown, however, that the child had been around for some time.

France was the first but not the only nation of Western Christianity to experience a special divine call to prominence among the Christian nations, and of course intentionally to the benefit of all of them. In the sixteenth century, a similar call was received by the Spain of Philip II. In the year of Philip's death, 1598, Tommaso Campanella, in his book on the Spanish monarchy, called the king of Spain the catholic king of the world commissioned to unify all mankind under the pope, in Europe as well as in America.[29] On the side of the Reformation, a similar function was increasingly attributed to England at that time. All these ideas, combining a particular nationality with a universal mission, had their element of truth. They all reflect, each under specific circumstances, the situation of a divided Christianity. They also reflect the responsibility, on occasion of historical opportunities, for restoring its unity and for vicariously taking care of the common responsibility of all Christianity in relation to mankind at large. Thus, in the context of the Christian tradition, nationalistic enthusiasm with its peculiar missionary zeal arose after the disintegration of the Christian empire in the West and aimed again and again at its restitution on the basis of the commitment of a particular nation. In consequence of the decomposition of the ancient Christian empire, but uneasy because of that memory, the Christian sense of chosenness to form one people under God was multiplied. It disintegrated into pieces; and each particular nation, when its time came, got the call to reintegrate the pieces and to restore the unity of all Christianity together with its mission to the rest of the world. A similar development happened, by the way, after the dissolution and downfall of the Eastern part of the former Christian empire, especially to Russia. After the fall of Byzantium, Russia took on its heritage and stylized its capital into the third Rome, the center for the completion of Christian history. Perhaps this dynamic has not altogether disappeared today, although in a secularized form it survives in the contemporary phenomenon of Russian revolutionary expansionism.

It is hardly necessary to mention the ambiguities in such emotional experiences of national chosenness. The call to serve the world was too often understood as a license for dominating one's neighbors. The consciousness of chosenness intensified national pride and appetite to such a degree that again and again antagonism among the Christian nations led to disastrous consequences. In the nineteenth century the missionary zeal connected with such nationalism had been civilized to some extent. Yet the irrational forces of nationalistic antagonism brought about the European catastrophe of World War I, thus revealing the disastrous consequences of the idolatrous perversion of the experience of a national calling.

Nevertheless, there is also a positive side to the belief in national chosenness. It has often been distinguished by an awareness and alertness to opportunities for being of service to mankind and, originally, of service to the Christian family of nations in order to reunite them as the people of God destined to bring peace and justice to all nations.

The most important and telling example in modern history of the more positive aspects in the experience of national chosenness has been England. English nationalism was characterized by a particularly close relationship to the Old Testament, perhaps plausible on the basis of the Biblicism of the late medieval period and of the Reformation. One of the first examples of an interpretation of English contemporary experience in the light of the Old Testament was given by John Lyly, who in 1580 praised God for taking special care of England "as of a new Israel, his chosen and peculiar people."[30] The appreciation of that divine providence was greatly enhanced after the almost miraculous redemption of England from the threat of the Spanish Armada in 1588. Such an experience inevitably evoked comparison with the miraculous redemption of Israel from their Egyptian persecutors at the Sea of Weeds. The climax of this tide of public piety was reached during the revolutionary wars of the seventeenth century. Oliver Cromwell himself was continuously looking for the finger of God in the events of his time. Unfortunately, all too easily he equated military victories with the divine confirmation of the cause of the victorious party. In 1653, in his first speech to Little Parliament, he told the new deputies, who were in fact his appointees, that they had been called by God himself in order to rule together with him and instead of him.[31] Most remarkable for this political theology, however, are a few sentences from a speech in 1657.[32] There, Cromwell wanted to bear testimony to the members of Parliament "that they have been zealous of the two greatest concernments that God hath in the world. The *one* is that of religion and of the just preservation of the professors of it; to give them all due and just liberty, and to assert the truth of God." This liberty Cromwell called "a catholic interest of the people of God." Then he continued: "The other thing cared for is the civil liberty and Interest of the nation. Which though it is, and indeed I think ought to be, subordinate to the more peculiar Interest of God,—yet it is the next best God hath given men in this world." And Cromwell concluded characteristically: "If any whosoever think the Interest of Christians and the Interest of the Nation inconsistent, or two different things, I wish my soul may never enter into their secrets." Both the greatness and the ambiguity of the English revolution and of its sense of chosenness are closely connected here. On the one hand, the principle of liberty, both religious and civil, constitutes indeed its great contribution to mankind. In this respect Cromwell's sense of chosenness was not altogether mistaken. But what he calls the interest of the nation, regarding it as closely connected with the issue of civil liberty, reminds one of all the cruelties of the revolutionary wars, especially in Ireland, where Cromwell had fought, as he reported back home, the battles of the Lord in order to communicate to the Irish people that English liberty which they would enjoy after they surrendered their weapons.[33]

A more detailed interpretation of the English revolution was offered by John Milton, its greatest apologist. In his pamphlet *The Tenure of Kings and Magistrates* (1649), in defending the deposition and decapitation of Charles I, Milton presented in a remarkable way the prospect of the revolution. He boldly argued that precisely because of the horrifying event of Charles's deposition and decapitation God would bless the English people, "calling us to liberty and to flourishing deeds of a reformed Commonwealth; with this hope that as God was heretofore angry with the Jews who rejected him and his forme of Government to choose a King, so that he will bless us, and be propitious to us who reject a King to make him onely our leader and supreme governour in the conformity as near as may be of his own ancient government."[34] Five years earlier, in his

Areopagitica (1644), Milton had indicated his conviction that England was moving ahead of other nations who would follow her attempt to establish a free society, and he identified this to be the continuation and completion of the Reformation: "Why else was this Nation chos'n before any other, that out of her as out of Sion should be proclaim'd and sounded forth the first tidings and trumpet of Reformation of all Europ. And had it not ben the obstinat perversnes of our Prelats against the divine and admirable spirit of Wicklif, to suppresse him as a schismatic and innovator, perhaps neither the Bohemian Husse and Jerom, no nor the name of Luther, or of Calvin had bin ever known: the glory of reforming all our neighbours had bin compleatly ours. . . . now once again by all concurrence of signs, and by the generall instinct of holy and devout men, as they daily and solemnly expresse their thoughts, God is decreeing to begin some new and great period in his Church, ev'n to the reforming of Reformation itself: what does he then but reveal Himself to his servants, and as his manner is, first to his Englishmen."[35] That completion of the Reformation, however, was expected by Milton to result from the realization of religious and civil liberty: "For now the time seems come, wherein Moses the great Prophet may sit in heav'n rejoycing to see that memorable and glorious wish of his fulfill'd, when not only our sev'nty Elders, but all the Lords people are become Prophets."[36] This fulfillment of Num. 11:29 meant, of course, that every individual would be immediate to God, as the prophets were by the presence of God's Spirit.

It would be unfair to belittle the obvious element of truth in this sense of historical destiny. The English revolution did indeed pioneer the political emancipation in the Western world, and there was not only a secular issue at stake but the social and political realization of the Christian freedom that had been reappropriated to the Christian consciousness by the Reformers.As a purely secular issue it was first considered in France, where people became enthusiastic about the English liberty but had to obtain it later without the support of a nonconformist version of Christianity. In its religious form,

however, the call to liberty and to the formation of a republic
of free men was passed on to England's American colonies
through the Pilgrim fathers and Puritans. Their sense of destiny could feed on the Old Testament to an even greater extent
than in England, since the emigrants to America could also
appropriate the theme of the exodus to the promised land and
of a new society built upon a divine covenant. It is not necessary to expound in detail how this sense of historical destiny
continued to be vigorous, in a more secular form during the
eighteenth century, but then again in the language of Christian
spirituality in the nineteenth century, culminating in the
thought of President Lincoln. It remains effective to the present day in the United States more than in any other Western
nation.

By way of a summary, this spirit has been expressed repeat-
edly in the context of inaugural addresses of American presi-
dents. It can be found in President Lyndon Johnson's inaugural
address. With reference to the American forefathers Johnson
said: "They came here . . . to find a place where a man could
be his own man. They made a covenant with this land. Conceived in justice, written in liberty, bound in union, it was
meant one day to inspire the hopes of all mankind, and it binds
us still. If we keep its terms, we shall flourish."[37] The use of
the idea of a covenant in this argument is revealing. In former
times it was God who made the covenant, not the American
forefathers. And the covenant was not made with the land, but
the land was given to the people of God on condition of their
faithful observance of the terms of God's covenant. Even in its
perversion, however, the use of religious language makes those
who speak that language vulnerable to the authentic meaning
of the words. It is more difficult for Christian theology to
criticize political claims that are no longer expressed in traditional Christian language.

The American sense of vocation and covenant is to be taken
just as seriously as earlier experiences of national vocation in
the course of Christian history. Today it is hard to tell to what
degree such statements express more than public rhetoric. But

basically, Christian theology should consider such a pledge to
be of positive value, because it renders the policies of a nation
accountable to the will of God as expressed in the Bible and
places the nation under the judgment of God. There are, of
course, the demons of nationalism around. That applies to the
United States as well as to other nations in Christian history.
As Richard Neuhaus recently stated:[38] "The idea that America
was a chosen people that could do no wrong was indeed a peril
to ourselves and others." But the complete disengagement of
political life from religious interpretation is no better than that
nationalistic perversion. Such a secular attitude, rather, indicates a refusal to relate one's own public life, its opportunities
and responsibilities, to the reality of the God who acts in
history. Thus Neuhaus is also right in his statement: "To assert
that America has been given less than it has been given is not
modesty but self-deceit. It is yet another instance of the desire
to escape from judgment."

The difficulty is how the accountability of a nation pledging
itself to a special vocation by the God of Israel revealed in Jesus
Christ is to be made concrete in such a way that it may be
discernible from self-legitimating political rhetoric. It is difficult to see how this can be done except by the prophetic
witness of the church, and most reliably by a united church
that is not confined within the limits of the national territory
and therefore not so easily deceived by national pride nor
one-sidedly preoccupied with issues of only regional importance. In short, it is the voice of a truly catholic church that
would be needed in order to check and to keep in its place the
claim of a particular nation to a divine vocation and mission.
To be theologically legitimate, however, such a claim has to be
related as well to the will of God to peace and justice among
all men as to the unity of the people of God in the process of
history. This unity may be conceived at present in cultural
more than in strictly political terms. Nevertheless it entails
specific political consequences and loyalties. Without restoring
a religious dimension even to questions of international politics
the claim of existing as a covenanted nation is not to be taken

seriously. But if it lives up to that claim, such a nation may contribute in an important way to a resurgence of the consciousness of all Christians to belong to one and the same people of God. At present they are divided politically as well as ecclesiastically. But they are still one in a communion that is not restricted to the spiritual domain of private faith and sharing in a common responsibility for peace and justice in all mankind.

It may be considered high time for the Christian churches and their theology to recognize the elements of corporate election and mission as well as of judgment in the political history of Christianity. It is urgent that they be redeemed from the ambiguities and perversions of their alienated persistence in the form of civil religions of particular nations. A reappropriation of the subject of historical corporate election of the people of God may also relieve the churches themselves of a narrowly ecclesiocentric perspective focusing exclusively on the church as an institution. And finally, a new sensibility for the divine election as relating to the people of God should open up the churches not only beyond national boundaries and beyond themselves as particular institutions. It should enable them to acknowledge the continuing claim of the Jewish people to be the people of God. To recognize the history of Christianity as an extension of the election and history of Israel would enable the Christian churches to get rid of their narrow exclusivism and would provide a basis for coping with the pluralistic situation of religion in modern society by looking beyond themselves to the purpose of God for all mankind.

5
Election and History

SINCE THE EIGHTEENTH CENTURY, HISTORY HAS BEEN CON-
ceived of as a continuous stream toward the progressive realization of humane standards of life. World history appeared as a
unified process, periodized by the succession of empires each
of which was born from a new people rising to historical prominence. In our century this concept has been abandoned. Instead, there has been general acceptance of the notion of a
plurality of cultures; and within the group of those twenty-one
cultures or civilizations—to use the figure of Arnold Toynbee
—the history of our Western culture represents only a comparatively small segment.

In a study of the history of Christianity, however, an important question arises. Is the concept of a culture or civilization
in fact adequate as it is usually accepted as basic unit of historical study? Cast in that language, Christian history began in
Hebrew and Hellenistic cultures, matured within the Roman
society, stretched out into Byzantine and medieval cultures,
and finally produced, or at least participated in producing, our
modern Western culture. The question seems inevitable: Is not
the overarching continuity of that process of Christian history
historically more important than the supposedly dividing lines
between those different civilizations in which Christian history
is believed to have successively participated? It was the Christian religion and church that transmitted the learning of classical antiquity to the medieval world, as well as secured for it the

continuous use of Roman law. And, most important, there was the institution of the Roman Catholic Church itself that continued from the ancient Roman period through the Middle Ages.

Arnold Toynbee suggested that there was a cultural watershed in the last quarter of the eighth century. Before 775 the scene had been dominated, even in its decay, by the Roman Empire, centered on the borders of the Mediterranean. After that year there emerged with the Frankish empire a new center in northern Europe.[39] For all the obvious suggestiveness of this argument, however, it seems that Toynbee overemphasized the shift in the political center and form of organization and underestimated the continuity represented basically by the Christian church. This element of the continuity makes it difficult to recognize at that point a radically new beginning of a completely new civilization. The notion of a line of inheritance that, according to Toynbee and others, links medieval culture to the Roman and Hellenistic civilizations seems too weak to account for the institutional as well as cultural continuity represented by the Christian church in the West. It is still more inadequate to account for the even stronger ties of Byzantine history with the Roman Empire. Also in Western culture, of course, the restoration of the Roman Empire in the Western part of its former territory continued to function as an important concern for many centuries. If, according to Toynbee, it would be artificial to insulate a national history such as the English from the context of Western culture,[40] then it is no less artificial to disregard the cultural, institutional, and religious links between the period of the Roman Empire and the new political structure that reached its first culmination with Charlemagne. It seems equally artificial to consider the continuity of religious institutions and traditions as something supercultural in order to save the assumption of a basically new civilization emerging with the Frankish empire.

It would be more appropriate to reconsider the question of what constitutes the basic units of history. Do civilizations in the sense of the recently accepted definition of that term really form those basic units of history? The case of Western history does not provide a particularly favorable example for that theory. It seems more natural to take the entire development of Christianity to represent one such historical unit. That would include not only Western history all the way through the modern period but also the Byzantine empire and the heirs of Byzantine culture, especially Russia. To make religion the fundamental issue in determining the basic units of history would also correspond to the assumption of modern sociological theory that religion in one form or another constitutes the basis of the social system.[41] Certainly, religion is not necessarily bound to a particular social system. The Christian religion became basic for different forms of social systems in the course of Christian history without being confined within their limits. On the other hand, religious continuity itself provides a degree of social and cultural continuity, since religion is concerned not only with another world but with a transcendent reality that constitutes the true meaning of precisely this present life and world.

The last consideration also makes understandable why religion was usually not considered as constitutive for the basic elements of history. Such a view, if taken seriously, would finally lead to a religious interpretation of history, e.g., to a theology of history. If the function of religion within the social system is due to the acceptance of a transcendent reality as constitutive of the true meaning of the present, then only in terms of that divine reality can the history of a society be accounted for. This is especially true with Christianity, as it is with the Jewish religion, because both rely on a God who reveals himself through his actions in history. In Jewish and Christian faith, history is explicitly an issue, while in mythological religions attention was turned away from the process of time and history and directed to a primordial past. Thus, if it is true in general that the history of society is to be understood in relation to its belief system concerning a transcendent reality that constitutes the meaning of the present, it is particularly true for Christianity and Judaism. These religions have interpreted not only the social system but also its history in religious terms. If the unity of Western history, transcending the epochal divisions between ancient, medieval, and modern periods, is provided by the continuity of the Christian tradition process, then that unity has to be described basically in religious terms. Such a description becomes in fact a theology of history—an interpretation of a divine activity in history. This explains the hesitation or unwillingness among secular historians to take religion seriously as a fundamental condition for unity in historical processes. As long as the basis of historical reality is seen in political and economic structures, religious belief can be treated as a secondary, if somewhat strange expression of those supposedly more basic social structures. Thus the transcendent reality to which religious belief is referring may be disregarded. But if religion itself is to be taken seriously as basic for the social system, and if, consequently, religious continuity provides continuity of other aspects of civilization and social life, then the question becomes urgent. Historical continuity (or discontinuity) must then be understood finally in religious terms.

It is important to notice that such an interpretation need not introduce supernatural categories into the description of historical events and processes. That of course has been the prevailing suspicion among historians. They fear interference of theology in the work of historical reconstruction. And that suspicion was not by any means without reason. It was quite appropriate in relation to premodern Christian theology. The characteristic claim of premodern Christianity to supernatural authority precluded any liability of its assertions to historical research and reflection, despite the fact that the basic affirmations of the Christian faith are concerned with historical events. The supernaturalism of traditional Christianity inevitably appeared to the modern mind as an arbitrary imposition upon empirical fact, especially upon historical judgment and reconstruction. With the beginning of modern times, the fundamental opposition of reason against authority was finally applied to history itself, a field that had been considered through many centuries a prerogative of authority. Thus, if religious or theological elements are to be reintroduced into the reconstruction and re-presentation of history, that cannot be done in terms of authoritative statements of faith that would not be open to critical historical examination. Such a thing had to be rejected by the historian as an arbitrary imposition on what he has to establish as historical fact. Nor is it advisable to reintroduce religious and theological categories into historical discourse in the milder form of some additional interpretation of facts the establishment of which would be left to the secular historian. Such a secondary interpretation, if not vulnerable to historical fact, would have to be rejected as an arbitrary addition that would be irrelevant to the task of the historian. Nor could such an arbitrary addition of some secondary interpretation of historical processes in religious terms satisfy the need of the Christian faith for a theological interpretation of history. Every serious theology of history refers to God as the determinative power active in historical reality, so that the process of history cannot be adequately or even appropriately understood without reference to God's action in history. No private and more or less arbitrary interpretation of history could achieve such an appreciation of God's activity as indispensable for an appropriate understanding of historical processes.

On the other hand, such a reference to God and his action need not be labeled "supernatural." This word would be inescapable only if the nature of historical reality were defined axiomatically in such a way as to exclude from the outset any reference to God as the unifying power in all reality. Such an axiomatic definition would seem to exhibit a prejudice rather than an attitude of critical rationality, and this kind of prejudice against religion has in fact prevented modern historical reconstruction from accounting for the unity of historical processes in accordance with the insights of contemporary sociology concerning the basic importance of religion for the social system. Of course, in dealing with history the reality of God cannot be simply presupposed. That also would amount to a prejudiced view. But in the reconstruction of historical processes the reality of God can and should be taken into account as a matter of dispute, not yet definitively settled but neither to be completely disregarded. Theological language need not represent an authoritarian or speculative imposition upon historical reality as critically established. Theological language can function in a descriptive way, open to examination and revision. The reasons for excluding religious language from historical discourse have been valid in relation to premodern authoritarian theology, but they do not necessarily apply in general.

The thesis of the following argument is that in the Biblical writings, especially in their reports of ancient Israelite history, the notions of God and of his actions in history functioned primarily in a descriptive way by providing a meaningful unity to historical experience. Certainly, the Biblical writings did not treat the reality of God explicitly as a matter of dispute. Nevertheless these reports demonstrate that the reality of the God of Israel was in fact in dispute in the course of the history they describe. This situation calls for an interpretation that makes explicit that openness of the Biblical language about God for the process of historical experience. That experience, of course, did not exclude in principle the presence of the Divine in ordinary reality but was, rather, extremely concerned with this particular aspect of reality at large.

A classic example from the Biblical writings for the descriptive attitude concerning history is found in one of the oldest historical accounts of the Bible, the story of how Solomon came to succeed to the throne of his father David. Here, it is only the failure of so many human political attempts that indicates the finger of God in the way he fulfilled the prophecy of Nathan to David assuring him of the continuous rule of his dynasty. The later examples of interpreting the course of history in relation to prophetic pronouncements are basically similar. The most important addition occurs in the category of judgment as explaining the deviation of history from the salutary aims originally intended in God's promises. In this language, the category of promise emphasizes possibilities of historical achievement that envision a creative lure for human action, while the category of judgment concerns the natural consequences inherent in human failure. It is important to realize that, according to the Biblical traditions, divine judgment is not imposed on the human reality of life from the outside, but spells out the intrinsic consequences of human behavior that does not care about God. The wrath of God, according to Paul (Rom. 1:24ff.), consists in leaving his creatures to the disastrous consequences of their own behavior. It is in the event of judgment that these consequences become apparent.

Neither the category of promise nor that of judgment, then, imports a supernatural interference of God with historical experience. Even the concept of miracle, though it is admittedly open to supernatural interpretation, does not necessitate it. A miracle is but an extraordinary event, and the occurrence of such an event is a question of historical experience and judgment and not necessarily of authority. Only when the occurrence of extraordinary events is affirmed on the basis of authority against rational inquiry does an opposition between theological and historical language become inevitable. In addition, the importance of miraculous actions of God in relation to a theology of history is easily overstated. To be sure, at least one such event, the resurrection of Jesus, should have a place of central importance in the Christian theology of history. However, its affirmation is not to be based on authority rather than on a critical evaluation of evidence. Nor does it provide a basic methodological category for a theology of history, as the notions of promise and judgment do.

The most fundamental category, however, in a theological description of history within the context of the Jewish-Christian tradition is the category of *election* as referring to the definitive intention in the corporate experience of the vocation of a people. The singularity of the elective act implied in that definitive intention precedes and underlies all the subsequent history of God's grace turned upon the people he chose once for himself. Thus the act of election constitutes the unity of that history, since it provides a continuous direction to the course of events. All the particular promises or admonitions arising subsequently from particular situations have their place within that history which was constituted by the act of election.

The same is true for the law of God which was given to keep the chosen people from falling into sin that would separate them from the grace and covenant of God. That law explicitly spells out the conditions of continuous persistence of the social community of the people as intended in the act of election itself. Thus in some way the law only specifies what is implicit in the act of election itself.

The act of election was identified in ancient Israel in different ways, but it was always understood as a unique act constituting the entire course of Israel's subsequent history. This uniqueness of the elective act did not preclude, however, the possibility of particular persons' or groups' being chosen in a particular way and to a particular function in the service of the people within the encompassing context of the history constituted once in the election of the people itself. Nor did the uniqueness of the elective act necessarily limit the concept of election to Israel in distinction from other nations. The particularity of Israel's existence as the chosen people of God was indeed bound up with its particular chosenness. Nevertheless the prophet Amos turned against the pride and complacency that arose from that experience and affirmed that God had his special histories with other nations too: " 'Are not you Israelites like Cushites to me?' says the Lord. 'Did I not bring Israel up from Egypt, the Philistines from Caphtor, the Aramaeans from Kir?' " (Amos 9:7). Thus, although many other Biblical texts stress the particularity of Israel's chosenness, that particularity is not completely without its parallels. This is important for the understanding of the descriptive character of the category of election. That category is related to the experience of a redemptive and foundational event that constitutes the further history of a people. Even Amos, however, would have had to acknowledge that only Israel explicitly worshiped Yahweh, although in fact he guided other nations in their histories as well.

This uniqueness of Israel, then, is itself a descriptive fact. In this sense, only Israel was the people of God, because those other nations did not worship Yahweh. The difference, then, between Israel and those other nations is explicable in purely descriptive terms. Even the notion of election, therefore, is not a supernatural term that would exempt the chosen one from the rest of reality. To the contrary, it is a descriptive notion available and applicable to ordinary experience though only under given conditions.

One could argue that in the Biblical traditions the implication of the reality of God in the notion of election was never in dispute and therefore it was a dogmatic and not a purely descriptive notion. Although this is true in regard to the explicit context of Biblical statements, it is not possible to understand the process of change in the transmission of Biblical traditions except on the assumption that the reality of Israel's God itself was again and again in dispute. Therefore, a contemporary interpretation has to treat such assertions of divine election as in fact hypothetical and to be tested against the ongoing process of Israel's experience. In addition, they have to be evaluated within the even more comprehensive horizon of an unfinished process of human history. Even today in that ongoing process of experience the question of the reality of God is not definitely settled.

To elucidate further the experiential character of the concept of election, that notion will be discussed henceforth in a generalized way. Although the concept is taken from ancient Israelite experience, it may be applicable to historical experience in general under comparable conditions.

The most basic contribution of the notion of election to a theology of history is that it provides some intelligible interpretation of statements affirming actions of God in history. It provides an interpretation that attributes to such religious language an explanatory function in relation to historical experience. In the first place, the term "election"—in relation to a people—is explanatory of the particular event or experience to which it refers. An experience of basic importance for the historical identity of a social unit is seen in connection with its adherence to a particular God and to a particular way of worshiping that God. That the formative events of a national history, if anything, are related to God—or, in more general terms, to the problematic dimension of divine reality—is no surprise. In the religious history of mankind the divine reality is generally understood as constitutive for the human world and, vice versa, the human world is understood as based upon that divine reality. The notion of election indicates further that it was the initiative of the God himself—and not just human initiative—that constituted the social world and the basically religious identity of a people. Some such emphasis on divine initiative is a self-evident implication of any employment of religious language in explaining historical experience. Therefore, this element again does not yet indicate the specific emphasis characteristic of the use of the term "election" in referring to such historical experience. The particular emphasis of that notion, in this respect, is that the divine initiative constitutive of the social world does not coincide with the cosmological origins of the natural world, but is seen as a contingent historical event. The notion of election, then, imports primarily the religious qualification of a historical experience of basic or foundational social importance. In such a way it is explanatory of that particular instance of experience.

In the second place, the notion of election suggests the evaluation of subsequent historical events and experiences in terms of their relationship to that formative phase of a historical process. The notion of election is related to foundational experiences of continuing relevance for the social unit concerned in spelling out their meaning that by far transcends the original occasion. Therefore future experiences will be understood in that perspective. That is, they too will be understood as actions of the God who created the meaningful unity of his chosen people and who faithfully carries on his gracious intentions for it. These intentions, in the first place, are concerned with the establishment and preservation of a social order as a condition for the continuous existence of the people. They are concerned therefore with the establishment of peace and justice, overcoming again and again the evil powers that threaten the survival of the chosen people. But not all historical experiences fit that model. The more unfortunate experiences of mischief and failure or even of historical disaster require additional principles of explanation. They may be attributed to some mythical origin in terms of a dualistic concept of evil powers fighting against the God who elected his people. Or they may in part be explained in terms of the behavior of the elected ones themselves in relation to the basic conditions of their communion with God, summarized in the principles of their social community. To the extent to which such explanations are possible, the misfortune that hits the people becomes explicable in terms of another action of God, as an occurrence of *judgment.* God's judgment reveals his power over those whose behavior is not in accordance with the order instituted by him for the well-being of his chosen people. The experience of judgment demonstrates that there is no escape from God's power for those who deviate from his purposes and show contempt for him instead of reverence and devotion. The notion of judgment, therefore, is the necessary supplement to the idea of election in a theology of history developed in terms of the pervasive activity of only one God in the course of historical events. When God seems absent not only from the world but from the hearts of human beings, this does not indicate, as a superficial evaluation would suggest, that perhaps he died. Rather, it foretells impending judgment over a world that alienated itself from the source of life.

Together, the two notions of election and judgment provide an explanation of historical experience in terms of God's action in the sequence of events. In this, the notion of judgment is dependent upon the idea of election. Only on the basis of the elective intention of God can experiences of misfortune and disaster become positively explicable as acts of the same God reacting against human contempt of his purposes and of his order of peace and justice entrusted to his chosen people. The notion of this order, then, which comprises the purposes of

God for the chosen people in the very act of his choosing and
spells out the conditions for its continuous social existence,
constitutes the third essential term of a theology of history. On
the basis of the notion of election, as of a foundational act of
God in history, the order of social existence is not traced back
to the cosmic order. Instead it is conceived in historical terms
as a *covenant* offered to the people at a particular moment in
history in connection with their election by God. The covenant
comprises all those conditions which the people pledge themselves to observe in committing themselves to serve the God
who chose them to exist as his people. The social order conceived of as a covenant is rooted in the elective act, but it
becomes also the basis of possible judgment. Since the people
are accountable to God on the basis of his covenant with them,
their failure to meet the conditions of the covenant provides
the reason for the occurrence of judgment. The idea of a
covenant renders the experience of judgment intelligible. Thus
it mediates between the notions of election and judgment in
a theology of history. The intention of the covenant, of course,
does not aim at judgment, but rather at vindication. It seeks
the vindication of God's purposes in history as well as the
vindication of the people whose existence is founded on their
election by God. The final vindication of God in history will
be the advent of his Kingdom which will bring about the full
realization of God's purposes as outlined in the scheme of his
covenant. Conversely, the divine covenant offered to a people
in the historical experience of chosenness is an anticipation of
that perfect human society, constituted in peace and justice,
which is to be expected only from the Kingdom of God himself
and not from any form of human government.

On the basis of these considerations, it may be apparent that
the notion of election, together with the notions of judgment
and covenant, can indeed provide a key to the interpretation
of historical expereince and heritage in theological terms. But
is it also applicable to the history of Christianity and Western
culture? If so, does it really function in opening up the details
as well as the unity of that historical process? Is it anything

more than a category of arbitrary interpretation, superimposed on the facts and thus finally superfluous in regard to the explanation of empirical phenomena?

The answer to these questions lies in the pervasive influence of the idea of election, or chosenness, in the history of Christianity. There was not only a theological doctrine of election but also a consciousness of chosenness that had its own history in Christianity, not only in the church but also in political history. In some cases the concept of chosenness served to legitimate historical processes that came originally from other than religious roots, as in the rise of the Constantinian empire. In other cases, especially in American history, the consciousness of chosenness and the close comparisons with ancient Israelite history seem to have had a formative influence on the course of historical events themselves. In the history of the British reformation, the consciousness of a peculiar chosenness apparently came rather late, toward the end of the sixteenth century. All the more powerful was its historical impact in the period of the British civil war of the seventeenth century. Another variation is exemplified by the course of early French history. The position of the early French kings was not first established, but decisively strengthened by the continuous claim to the heritage of Charlemagne and by the pope's special recognition of the French king and people. Both involved a consciousness of peculiar chosenness. In German medieval history there seem to be no comparable expressions of a claim to peculiar national chosenness. That may be due to the fact that the German king was more or less universally recognized as carrying on the imperial ministry and authority of Charlemagne and of the ancient Roman emperors. The presence of that universal office, universal at least in its intentions and in its recognized dignity, was at the same time a matter of national pride. Yet it prevented the development of a particularly national identity and consciousness of chosenness. This may explain why German nationalism entered the scene of history comparatively late, at the beginning of the nineteenth century when the fiction of the medieval empire finally came to an end. But even then in

German nationalism the religious element, in a romantic fashion, was still rather strong.

Notwithstanding all those differences in the ways a consciousness of chosenness became effective in Western history, it is obviously not a category superimposed by subsequent interpretation while foreign to the empirical facts themselves. The nature of its impact was different on different occasions. This argument does not plead for a view of history as created by human ideas and visions alone. But the consciousness of chosenness was continuously a factor of great importance in the history of Christianity, producing historical effects in some cases and, even more important, integrating historical experience in others. The decisive question, of course, is whether it was and is only an element of human consciousness, without objective validity; or whether that consciousness of chosenness expresses an awareness of special historical opportunity and responsibility appropriately to be explained only in religious terms, an awareness that may be as realistic as any factual knowledge.

The previous discussion of the experiential meaning of the category of election suggests that, indeed, one should take seriously the claim to peculiar chosenness in its many forms throughout Christian history. That does not oblige anybody to accept the overstatements of national pride and exclusivism. But from the Constantinian empire to the rise of Charlemagne and in the sequence of conceptions of a peculiar national chosenness in Western history, it can be shown that the consciousness of chosenness expresses and articulates a specific awareness of special historical opportunity and responsibility. This awareness is related to the God who revealed himself in the history of Israel and in Jesus Christ. We may quarrel with some details in the appraisal of the historical situation or, even more so, with the perception of particular responsibilities derived from it. But by and large, overall appraisals of the significance of historical situations, such as that of the Constantinian epoch by Eusebius or of the Cromwellian era by Milton, are remarkable for the degree of their accuracy. Even to the Puritans' awareness of a peculiar chosenness one should not deny a considerable degree of historical truth in spite of the narrowness of their Biblical legalism. In questions concerning the far-reaching significance of a specific history of one's own contemporary experience, the occurrence of misjudgments is not surprising. Much more surprising is the occurrence of accounts that one has to credit even today as largely appropriate. That religious sensitivity enabled some men to appraise their own situation in terms so highly accurate should be considered admirable.

In relating such an awareness of historical particularity to the God of the Bible, I cannot discover a basic element of idolatry. To the contrary, this phenomenon expresses in the first place the perhaps quite sincere piety of people who experience the concrete course of their own history in relation to the God whom they confess to act in history. On the basis of the election of Israel and of its extension to the Gentiles through the ministry of Christ, especially through his death and resurrection, such claims to particular chosenness in Christianity are less strange in principle than has often been assumed. There is nothing unbiblical in listening to the call of God in one's own personal and social history as long as one remains conscious of one's possible judgment. Much more awkward is a pretendedly Christian perspective that restricts the notion of election to a purely spiritual community. Such a view should be considered strange, since it shows itself to be overly dependent on secularist definitions of historical reality and no longer subordinates one's own social life and history to the theocratic claim of the God of the Bible. The inherent dangers in any claim to chosenness are obvious. They are essentially the same as in the history of ancient Israel—pride, exclusivism, presumptuous security, and contempt of possible or even impending judgment. But these dangers do not render the claim to chosenness illegitimate. *They are taken care of by the category of judgment.* By its claim to chosenness a group places itself under God's judgment in a specific way because it pledges itself to the will and purpose of God in history. Thus it makes itself accountable to the terms of God's covenant.

The covenantal element implicit in the pledge of chosenness, as it occurs in the context of Jewish and Christian history, cannot be completely extravagant in content without becoming self-contradictory. If the consciousness of chosenness refers to the God of the Hebrew Bible and of his revelation in Christ, all claims to a position of specific chosenness have to conform to the Biblical traditions of God's law and promise. They have to legitimate themselves by calling upon the Christological foundation of the Christian extension of the notion of the people of God to the Gentiles. Claims to a specific chosenness within the context of Christian history have to relate to the more comprehensive context of the eschatological people of God, comprising all of Christianity together with the Jewish people. Otherwise such claims would become self-contradictory in calling upon the God of Jewish and Christian history.

Thus, election and chosenness within the context of Christian history cannot be considered as positing a new people of God that would abandon and replace the old one. The eschatologically universal community of Christianity is no less irreplaceable than the Jewish people. As Christianity has to be understood in continuity with the election of the Jewish people in terms of the eschatological extension of Israel's election to the Gentiles, so the experience of a peculiar chosenness within Christianity cannot transcend the eschatological universality of the Kingdom of God symbolized in the Christian community. It can serve to further that purpose only on the basis of the specific historical opportunity of particular groups or nations within the context of Christianity.

The Christian community is constituted by the communion of every believer with Jesus Christ, a communion that unites the faithful among themselves. The ultimate foundation of that community, however, is the Kingdom of God that became present in the mission of the Messiah, Jesus Christ, and thus is present through Christ in the Christian community. This does not mean that the Christian church would be identical with the Kingdom of God. God's Kingdom becomes present in the church through his Spirit only if the church does not identify itself with the Kingdom. Precisely as Jesus distinguished himself from the father as a mere human being, he was in fact united with the Father in being the eternal Son. The community of the Christians is only symbolizing at present the eschatological community of a new mankind in the Kingdom of God. The divine Kingdom surpasses Christianity, and this difference between the two is constitutive of a possible symbolic function of the Christian community in relation to that eschatological future of mankind at large. Conversely, the identity of the Christian community is dependent on its testimony to the destination of all mankind in the Kingdom of God as it was proclaimed by Jesus Christ. In distinction from the Jewish community, eschatology, being a late development in Jewish thought, has become basic for the covenantal foundation of Christianity, since Jesus reinterpreted the sacred law of Israel in terms of the conditions implicit in the Kingdom of God that he proclaimed. All these conditions are summarized in the love of God claiming our life as it was symbolized by Jesus himself through his ministry and especially through his death. In the life of the church this covenantal basis of the church's existence is present in the symbolic action of the Eucharist, which commemorates the love of God in the death of Jesus and celebrates at the same time God's Kingdom to come, as Jesus did, in the image of the meal.

The symbolic representation of God's Kingdom to come has been the basic idea of Christian history. The entire course of that history is characterized by a continuous struggle for the expression of God's Kingdom in the life of the Christian people. It has been a struggle to reshape the society formed by Christians so as to correspond to their faith in the Kingdom of God. This applies to the Byzantine empire as well as to the medieval church in its relation to the political powers of that time. On the other side, it is exemplified by the Christian kingdoms and by the attempts to restore the Roman Empire in Western Christianity throughout the medieval period. The same principle even applies to the rise of modern Western culture after the period of confessional wars in Europe. When monarchical rule was abolished in England, that was legitimated by calling upon the direct rule of God himself. The idea of political freedom was based upon that direct and immediate relationship of each individual citizen to God and his rule. In modern constitutional government still the division of power testifies to the conviction that unlimited sovereignty belongs only to God.

In one of the most profound modern interpretations of Western history, Hegel asserted that the idea of freedom and the realization of that idea govern the entire course of Christian history—and even all of the world's history. That is an extremely suggestive and fascinating vision, and particularly so because it intimates to modern man that the specific experience of his own epoch was operative in history all along. But precisely this strength of Hegel's interpretation also reveals its limitations: Did he not read the modern experience into the earlier epochs of history? Today it seems more sober to identify the most general and recurrent theme of human history with Eric Voegelin in the contest and struggle for the true order of society rather than in the idea of individual freedom.[42] It was not until the modern period that the principle of individual freedom was made the criterion for the true order of society. Although the notion of freedom was basic in the Christian concept of salvation as presented in the New Testament, especially by Paul and John, it did not become a principle of political reconstruction before the modern period. Rather, the question of how the rule of God and the Kingdom of Christ were to be represented on earth determined the meaning structure of the social and political system during the ancient and medieval periods of Christian history. Only when the principle of the human mediation of God's rule by analogical representation lost its power in the minds of people, and instead the immediacy of each individual to God by faith was discovered, only then the rule of God was thought to exclude human mediation so that the independence of the individual from all human authority would correspond to his devotion to the rule of God alone.

This modern conception, however, for all its greatness has

been excessively individualistic. It simply presupposes that all human individuals according to their natural condition would live in basic harmony with God's rule and with the social purpose of his Kingdom. This presupposition was taken for granted in the course of modern history to the extent that the notion of God's rule and Kingdom later on could be replaced altogether by the notion of human nature. But today we perceive with greater clarity the delusive element in that presupposition. The immediacy of the individual to God, the unalienable rights of the individual in questions of ultimate truth, should certainly be preserved. Still the order of society is obviously not yet settled thereby. The question poses itself conversely: What sort of social order is fit to secure a maximum chance of individual immediacy to God, of individual freedom? Thus the issue of a social order in peace and justice corresponding to the Kingdom of God reemerges as the basic issue in history. It is basic also for the protection of individual freedom.

In Christian history the social system has been conceived of, not as representing the primordial order of the cosmos, nor in terms of a positive law, but as anticipating the eschatological Kingdom of God which is to transform this present world. Therefore, Christian history is characterized by an institutional distinction. The political order represents the future destiny of social life in the Kingdom of God under the present conditions of the social system. The religious institution of the church reminds the political order of its provisional nature in contrast to the ultimacy of God's eschatological future. Thus, by the ministry of the church, the truth embodied in the political order is redeemed by sublimation into symbolism, just as in the life of the church the Kingdom of God is present in the form of its symbolic celebration in memory of Christ.

The Christian people, chosen from all nations, has been elected to exist in this world as the eschatological community of the God of Israel and witnesses even now to his imminent rule over all his creation and over all mankind. This witness embodies a twofold symbolism: that exhibited within the life of the church; and that which emerges from the transformation of society into a provisional symbol of God's Kingdom to come through Christian criticism of the social structures in their self-affirming form. In the history of Christianity this witness has taken on different forms that constitute character- istics of the succeeding period of that history. Each period also involves particular forms of temptation and, correspondingly, of God's judgment in history. The periods of the history of Christianity, however, do not succeed each other in a unilinear way. The process of Christian history did not develop in a unilinear way because of the divisions that occurred in Christi- anity. Consequently the periods of that history overlap in part rather than forming a pure sequence.

The first period in the history of Christianity was that of the Christian empire. It began with opposing the imperial rule of the Roman emperor in favor of the rule of Christ. It continued with the submission of the emperor under the rule of Christ. The two phases of the history of ancient Christianity before and after the fourth century are not as starkly different in this respect as often has been assumed. They are governed by one and the same principle, the direct application of the rule of Christ, the heavenly king, to the administration of society. The predominant temptation of this period was the exclusivism of the Christian sense of chosenness, first visible in the relation- ship of Christianity to the Jewish people, who were no longer recognized as the people of God. Later on, the universalism of the Byzantine empire itself was perverted into exclusivism, especially by imperial insistence on dogmatic uniformity. The judgment of God on that perversion of the Christian vocation was specifically spelled out in the rise of Islam. The easy con- quest by the Islamic forces of the provinces in which Christian- ity had originated—Palestine and Syria—and subsequently Egypt and North Africa is not understandable apart from the alienation of these provinces from Byzantium in consequence of the imperial efforts to enforce dogmatic uniformity upon them, especially the acceptance of the Formula of Chalcedon in 451.

The second period in Christian history was that of the superiority of the church in determining the Christian identity of the social system. While in the Byzantine empire the difference between the eschatological Kingdom of God, symbolized in the life of the church, and the temporal and temporary rule of the emperor had been underestimated, the medieval church considered itself the temporal representation of the Kingdom of God and therefore tended also to dominate the political scene, since only by submission to the pope the Christian identity of society seemed to be warranted. Thereby the Christian church turned its spiritual symbolism into a legal structure of hierarchical order that claimed finally to encompass and penetrate all the dimensions of human life. The dogmatic exclusivism of the Christian sense of chosenness was continued in this period on the basis of medieval clericalism. God's judgment on that deformation of his church occurred in the divisions of the church. The most important for the Western world were the divisions that developed from the Reformation of the sixteenth century. These led to the period of confessional wars that became the threshold of the modern era.[43]

The modern era has been the period of a Christian culture. The Kingdom of God was no longer seen in the image of a universal peace to be achieved by a Christian empire that would unite all Christians. The contesting and mutually exclusive claims of the confessional churches had to be reduced to a matter of only private concern, lest they would continue to disrupt the social system. In consequence of the bracketing of confessional positions and differences, the unifying spirit of social life became secular. This did not necessarily mean that it became unchristian—but it became at least ambiguous. The Christian element in the roots of modern culture was no longer clearly identified as Christian, since the divided churches continued to exist as the only institutions to determine such Christian identity. Nevertheless, the principle of religious and political liberty, the basic principle of modern culture, could be understood—and has been understood—as representing the most universal and concrete realization so far of the Christian faith in human life. In contrast to the particularism of the

confessional churches disproving each other by their narrow
dogmatism, the principle of religious and political freedom
could be taken as the universally valid expression of that Christian freedom which the Reformers had identified as characterizing the very essence of the Christian faith. But even the
persistent existence of a secular society itself seems to be dependent on the continuing presence of the Christian religion
in modern society. Without the continuous presence of the
Christian churches, modern society might have been resacral-
ized long since, because the foundation for the unity of the
social system is inevitably religious or quasi-religious. Therefore, the modern period in the history of Christianity may be
duly characterized as the period of the Christian culture.

The ambiguity of the secularized idea of freedom, however,
required additional principles for the organization of modern
society. The most important one has been nationalism. Although modern nationalism, as well as liberalism, had its roots
in Christian history, in a history of experiences of corporate
chosenness, nationalism became in modern times as ambiguous
as liberalism in relation to those historical roots. While liberalism tended to legitimate either self-idolatrous individualism or
abstract equality—as implied in the universal character of the
liberty affirmed—nationalism became even more unabashedly
idolatrous. Judgment on the pride of nationalism is already
visible in the history of this century. It came to expression most
clearly in the self-destructive outburst of antagonisms of European nationalism in World War I that put an end to the
dominating role of Europe in the world. It meant that the
divine vocation that was perceived earlier in experiences of
national chosenness, had been forfeited by nationalistic self-
glorification. That judgment became definitive with World
War II. Among the hardest hit was the German nation. The
single most serious reason for that in theological as well as in
historical terms may have been the persecution and attempted
annihilation of the Jewish people. This attempt disclosed to
the world the radical nature of that nationalism. The German
case demonstrated in a particularly incisive way the dangerous

potential of nationalism, but it is uncertain whether the general significance of that experience has yet been properly understood in the contemporary world.

The catastrophe of European nationalism did not yet close the scene upon the modern epoch. This is still the hour of the principle of liberty and of a continuous calling for its realization in all dimensions of human life. But the ambiguities of its secular conception deprived the idea of liberty of its holistic meaning to such an extent that judgment on the societies based on that principle is already looming on the horizon. This judgment obviously appears in the rise of socialism. This ambiguous word may be taken as referring to the subordination in principle of the individual under some accepted image of society. If Western culture does not reappropriate the religious roots of its vision of freedom together with a more holistic reinterpretation of society, then its own people—and especially the younger generation—will cry out for socialism because they less and less will be able and willing to stand the meaninglessness of public life. Such a development would not put an end to the history of Christianity. The concern for the true order of society will continue under conditions of socialism and produce an increasing awareness of the ultimately religious foundation of social life. But the great experiment of developing an order of society on the basis of the idea of individual freedom would have become a past attempt that would have been disproved by the course of history.

Postscript

THE ABSTRACT INDIVIDUALISM CHARACTERISTIC OF THE CLASSI-cal Christian doctrine of election has been criticized in this book. The place of the individual in the framework of a redefinition of election in terms of a communal and historical process remains an important question. The question should be felt all the more urgent in view of what has been said, in the first chapter, about the eternal value of the individual as a crucial contribution of the Christian faith to the understanding of human existence. Interestingly enough, it was the same development that, starting from postexilic Jewish thought, produced both a new awareness of the destiny of the human individual beyond death to eternal community with God and the abstraction of individual election from the historical process of the people of God and from its mission in human history. The same development that resulted in a breakthrough to a new conception of the human dignity of individual existence on the basis of the individual's faithful adherence to God was accompanied by a tendency to recede from history into the seclusion of sectarian groups of true believers who considered themselves exclusively chosen by God from eternity to participate in his eternal glory, whatever course history might take.

The emphasis on the eternal value of the individual reached its very peak in Jesus' proclamation of the love of God for the sinner. At the same time, he broke the trend toward sectarian seclusion by returning from the desert to the villages of Galilee.

In his entire mission Jesus understood himself as being sent to all the people of Israel, an idea that found expression in the symbolic act of choósing twelve disciples corresponding to the twelve tribes of Israel. This comprehensive tendency—comprehensive as compared to the sectarian seclusion characteristic of so much of Jewish piety of that time—was further extended by the early Christian decision to carry the missionary proclamation of the risen Lord to the Gentiles, since in Jesus' resurrection the endtime had already dawned, when the Gentiles would turn to the God of Israel.

While Jesus did not establish a sect of his own—he did not in that sense become the founder of the church—yet he gathered the symbolic circle of the twelve and practiced the symbolic celebration of the Kingdom to come in the community of a meal. Both of these actions were comprehensive in their symbolism: the first in reference to all the people of Israel, the second even more so by representing the universal communion of a renewed humankind in the Kingdom of God. It was only after the crucifixion of Jesus that the Christians were forced to build a particular sect within the Jewish people and—because of the increasing weight of Gentile membership—increasingly in distinction from the Jewish people. Because of its eschatological symbolism, however, the Christian church did not become merely a particular community built upon the association of its individual members. Rather, it became an open and "catholic" community symbolizing the destiny of all humankind.

In the Christian community, it is not by natural propagation —as with the Jewish people—that an individual becomes a member of the people of God. Participation in the Kingdom of God is a matter, not of natural birth, but of spiritual rebirth. Thus the notion of individual faith is indeed fundamental in the concept of the church. Therefore the church as the assembly of the faithful is not simply identical with the historical people of God. On the one hand it is restricted to a remnant of that people, while on the other it extends beyond the natural limits of the chosen nation. Individual calling and election became and remains basic in the Christian community in a different way than in the case of the Jewish people. They have been chosen as a people without special attention to individual descendants of Abraham and Jacob. There was an important element of truth in the postexilic idea of election that even in choosing a nation God intended the conversion and salvation of individuals. The question is, who are the true descendants of Abraham? It sounds familiar to the reader of Paul's letters. But in the case of the Christians, the individuals were not chosen as a righteous remnant of the people because of their own righteousness, but to serve the purpose of God in his history with all mankind as has been the case with the people of Israel itself.

The intention of God's elective activity in human history is not limited to a particular community, nor to isolated individuals. The love of God is directed to mankind as symbolized in the life of individuals and to individual human beings embodying in their lives the destiny of all humanity. Therefore, individual men and women are chosen by God, but not as isolated atoms of salvation. They are chosen to exemplify the gracious intentions of God's love for all human beings. Hence, there is no room for sectarian seclusion of the chosen. Such elitist exclusivism only renders the excluded ones the more suitable examples of God's elective love.

The symbolic purpose in being chosen, however, constitutes a particular history of those who accept the call. In the case of the Christians, the election of the individual does not abolish the idea of a chosen people and its history. Instead it started a new historical process in the continuation of the election of Israel, in the continuation of the function of the chosen people in representing to the present world the destiny of all mankind in the future of God's Kingdom. Individual Christians of later generations cannot disregard this function of the Christian community and the particular shape it has taken in the ongoing process of its history without surrendering their Christian identity. Again and again, individual Christians enter into the continuing history and mission of Christianity. They have to stand up to the heritage of Christian history, taking upon themselves the burden of the divisiveness and distortions that resulted from that history. At the same time, they must listen to the call that was received by past epochs and still points beyond their failure, thus illuminating the contours and responsibilities of the present situation.

Notes

1. Cf. Gerhard von Rad, *Theologie des Alten Testaments*, Vol. I (1957), pp. 389ff.
2. This transition was described by R. H. Charles, *Eschatology: The Doctrine of a Future Life in Israel, Judaism and Christianity* (1899) (New York: Schocken Book 49, 1963), pp. 61ff.
3. Cf. Karlheinz Müller, "Die Ansätze der Apokalyptik," in J. Meier and J. Schreiner, *Literatur und Religion des Frühjudentums* (Würzburg, 1973), pp. 31–42.
4. E. Käsemann, *An die Römer*, Handbuch zum Neuen Testament 8a (Tübingen, 1973), pp. 280ff. See also p. 296, where Käsemann, however, still speaks of an idea of a "new" people of God as conceived by Paul, although he recognizes the function of the idea of the church as the people of God in characterizing "the phenomenon of the church according to its historical continuity."
5. A. Hamel, *Kirche bei Hippolyt von Rom* (Gütersloh, 1950), pp. 23ff. See also pp. 36ff. on the preparation of the position of Hippolytus by his teacher Irenaeus (e.g., IV.21.3). A first hint was given by Justin, *Dial.* 123.6f.
6. According to J. Ratzinger, *Volk und Haus Gottes in Augustins Lehre von der Kirche* (Munich, 1954), pp. 252ff., the use of this idea faded in post-Augustinian time. See also M. Schmaus, *Katholische Dogmatik* III/1 (1958), p. 231, and the sketch of the history of the idea, pp. 219–231. Schmaus thinks, however, that the idea of the church as *new* people of God was current in the New Testament (pp. 214ff., esp. p. 217).
7. The Second Assembly of the World Council of Churches, at Evanston (1954), spoke of the church as the "new people of God" without clear awareness of the problems entailed in such language concerning the relationship of the church to Israel. The Conference of the Commission on Faith and Order at Bristol (1967) still claimed, while the problem was felt more distinctly, the exclusive right of the church to the title of the eschatological people of God (cf. E. Dinkler, in Ökumenische Rundschau 17, 1968, pp. 285f.).

8. *Lumen Gentium* 2; cf. M. Keller, *"Volk Gottes" als Kirchenbegriff* (Zurich, 1970).
9. *Lumen Gentium* 2. 13: *"Ecclesia seu Populus Dei."* The idea of the church as a *new* people of God *(Lumen Gentium* 2.9: *"novus Populus Dei")* in distinction from Israel does not occur in the New Testament, but first in Barn. 5.7; 7.5.
10. Eusebius, *Hist. eccl.* I.4.2, ed. by E. Schwartz (1907), p. 14. Here Eusebius uses the term *ethnos,* which had been used sometimes by the LXX in a similar way as *laos,* to designate the chosen people of Israel, e.g., Ex. 19:6. This phrase was quoted by I Peter 2:9 as referring to the Christian community. The term *laos* is used elsewhere by Eusebius in the more indeterminate sense of "people" (X.4.63; Schwartz 385, 17). In the same way it occurs in an interesting phrase from a document of the emperor Constantine himself which is transmitted by Eusebius in Bk. X.6. There Constantine speaks of "the people of the holy and catholic church" that should not be deceived (Schwartz 394, 18f.).
11. Hippolytus of Rome, *Commentary on Daniel* IV.9 (*GCS,* Hippolyt I.1, pp. 206ff.). See the comments of H. Rahner, *Kirche und Staat im frühen Christentum* (Munich, 1961), pp. 24f.
12. Origen, *Contra Celsum* 2.30 (*GCS,* Vol. I, ed. by Koetschau, 1899, p. 158, 2ff.). On this passage, see the remarks of E. Peterson, *Kaiser Augustus im Urteil des antiken Christentums. Ein Beitrag zur Geschichte der politischen Theologie,* in *Hochland,* Vol. 30 (1932/33), pp. 289ff., esp. pp. 291f.
13. Eusebius, *Praep. ev.* I.4.9f. See also E. Peterson, *Der Monotheismus als politisches Problem. Ein Beitrag zur Geschichte der politischen Theologie im Imperium Romanum* (1935; reprinted in Theologische Traktate, Munich, 1951), pp. 49ff., esp. pp. 86ff. For the influence of Eusebius' ideas in the West, see F. Klingner, "Rom als Idee," in *Römische Geisteswelt* (1943), pp. 434ff., esp. pp. 452ff. (on Prudentius), but also Peterson, *Der Monotheismus,* pp. 95ff. (on Prudentius, Ambrosius, Hieronymus, Orosius). Peterson's criticism of these ideas by reference to the Arians and to their preference for the idea of divine monarchy (pp. 101ff.) does not seem convincing, since the trinitarian faith did not abandon the idea of divine unity.
14. Eusebius, *Praep. ev.* I.6ff.
15. Hans von Campenhausen, "Augustin und der Fall von Rom" (1946), in *Weltgeschichte und Gottesgericht* (1947), esp. p. 4. More recently, Jean-Claude Guy, *Unité et structure logique de la "Cité de Dieu" de saint Augustin* (Paris, 1961), argued against the assumption that the *City of God* was written *"uniquement comme un plaidoyer composé pour laver les chrétiens de la responsabilité qu'on leur imputait injustement de la ruine de Rome"* (p. 6), because only one out of twenty-two books treats that question extensively. Even the more modest thesis that Augustine wanted to restore to the Christian people its courage by demonstrating that the disaster of Rome was an event of only relative importance and did not touch the religious truth does

not meet Guy's full approval (p. 7). His own explanation, however, that the conquering of Rome served only as a starting point for Augustine's comprehensive critique of paganism and positive presentation of the mystery of the city of God (p. 10) seems to underestimate the constitutive importance of Augustine's negative judgment on pagan and Christian political theology for his own conception of the City of God. This connection was more accurately emphasized by von Campenhausen, but also by F. G. Maier, *Augustin und das antike Rom* (Stuttgart, 1955), pp. 76ff., esp. p. 78.

16. U. Duchrow, *Christenheit und Weltverantwortung* (1970), pp. 268ff., emphasizes with J. Straub (1954) the importance of the idea of terrestrial peace in Augustine's political thought, with special attention to Ep. 138 (281ff.). But even so he has to admit that in Augustine's perspective it is finally the peace of Babylon (pp. 314, 317) and not so much a positive analogy to the celestial peace in the Kingdom of God (*De civ. Dei* XV.13), but its Satanic imitation (cf. W. Kamlah, *Christentum und Geschichtlichkeit. Untersuchungen zur Entstehung des Christentums und zu Augustins "Bürgerschaft Gottes"* [Stuttgart, 1951], pp. 166ff., esp. pp. 171f., and also F. G. Maier, *Augustin und das antike Rom*, pp. 152ff., esp. pp. 164f. and pp. 182ff.). His qualification of Rome seems to follow the Western tradition expressed in Hippolytus rather than the Eastern one that developed from Melito and Origen to Eusebius. On Augustine's opposition to Eusebius and his followers, see Kamlah, pp. 176ff. His accusation against this theology as well as against pagan patriotism is concentrated in the statement of his sermon 105 (dating from 410): *"Terreno regno aeternitas adulatorie promissa"* (n. 10).

17. On this much-debated chapter, see A. von Harnack, *Dogmengeschichte*, Vol. III, 5th ed. (Tübingen, 1932), pp. 150ff., and the criticism of W. Kamlah, "Ecclesia und regnum Dei bei Augustin," *Philologus*, Vol. 93 (1938), pp. 248ff., summarized also in his *Christentum und Geschichtlichkeit*, pp. 140ff., 158ff. It is true that Augustine recognized a difference between the present form of the church and its future perfection. But the future *civitas* and the *peregrina civitas regis Christi* (*De civ. Dei* I.35; V.16) are basically the same reality. The eschatological element in Augustine's thought is overemphasized when the identification of the present church with the Kingdom of God (as it is represented at present) is reduced to a mere "anticipation" of the future Kingdom (Duchrow, p. 264).

18. See the balanced judgment of Hans von Campenhausen, *Lateinische Kirchenväter* (Stuttgart, 1960), p. 202.

19. In its beginnings this complicated process was furthered by the Roman see itself. The famous letter of Gelasius I to Emperor Anastasius in 494 on the difference and relationship between pontifical authority and *regalis potestas* (cf. E. Caspar, *Geschichte des Papsttums*, Vol. II (Tübingen, 1933), pp. 65ff., still presupposed the unity of the Empire, although following the example of Ambrosius and the thought of Augustine, it secularized the

character of the imperial authority. The renewal of the imperial authority. Three centuries later, during the icono-clastic quarrels, the papacy favored a renewal of the imperial authority in the West, certainly in spiritual subordination to Rome, but necessary for the protection of the Roman Church even against Byzantine encroachment on territories of papal jurisdiction in Italy since Leo III. The renewal of the imperial dignity, however, meant also a renaissance of Byzantine political ideas in the West, especially concerning the spiritual character of the imperial office as well as that of the king.

20. H. Löwe, *Von Theoderich dem Grossen zu Karl dem Grossen* (Darmstadt, 1956), esp. pp. 41ff.

21. The hotly debated question as to the character of that event at Christmas in 800 has been brought to a balanced conclusion by Peter Classen, "Karl der Grosse, das Papsttum und Byzanz. Die Begründung des karolingischen Kaisertums," in *Karl der Grosse, Lebenswerk und Nachleben*, Vol.I of Persönlichkeit und Geschichte, ed. by H. Beumann (Düsseldorf, 1967), pp. 537–608. Classen argues convincingly that Charlemagne was not taken by surprise by the pope. A prior agreement seems more likely (pp. 574ff.). See also F. L. Ganshof, "The Imperial Coronation of Charlemagne: Theories and Facts," in his book, *The Carolingians and the Frankish Monarchy* (London: Longmans, 1971), pp. 41ff., esp. p. 47. Ganshof has been criticized, however, by Classen for overestimating the role of Alcuin.

22. Classen, p. 604. The coronation had been a serious provocation of the Byzantine empire that regarded Charlemagne as usurper (Classen, p. 593) and Pope Leo as traitor who had separated himself from the empire by that act (p. 598). Therefore it was a remarkable success that finally, in 812, the emperor Michael through his special envoy gave Charlemagne the title and honor of an emperor, although in Byzantine perspective this did not involve full equality (W. Ohnsorge, *Das Zweikaiserproblem im frühen Mittelalter. Die Bedeutung des byzantinischen Reiches für die Entwicklung der Staatsidee in Europa* (Hildesheim, 1947), p. 29. Charlemagne, on his part, in a famous letter of 813 addressed Michael as emperor and augustus—the same titles he used for introducing himself. In addition, he expressed his claim to equality by calling the Byzantine emperor "brother" (*Monumenta Germaniae historica epistolarum*, Vol. IV, ed. by E. Dümmler [Berlin, 1895], p. 556). At the same time, Charlemagne avoided any reference to the "Roman" character of his imperial authority (Classen, p. 603), but rather expressed his desire for stabilizing the peace *"inter orientale atque occidentale imperium"* and for protecting the church *"quae toto orbe diffusa est."*

23. As early as 794/95 Alcuin in one of his letters wrote that Charlemagne was elected by God, as David in former times had been, in order to guide and teach his people: *"(Christ) David regem populo suo concessit rectorem et doctorem"* (Ep. 41, Dümmler, Vol. IV, p. 84). Later on, Alcuin regularly addressed Charlemagne as David and as chosen by God (e.g., Ep. 148, *ibid.*, p. 237, 27). In connection with the neo-adoptionist quarrel, he called on his

king as "chosen man" and son of God *(filius Dei)* against the Spanish bishop Felix of Urgel that he should act before that heresy would be spread *per orbem christiani imperii.* This argument suggests that two years later (June, 800) the exhortation to protect *christiani imperii pacem* (Ep. 201, p. 336, 26) also refers to the Christian Roman empire, as Ganshof (p. 34) suggests (cf. p. 33), contrary to Classen, who denies a political connotation of that phrase (p. 571).

24. See E. Eichmann, *Kirche und Staat* I (Munich, 1968), 60, 12 *(cuius typum geris in nomine),* cf. 73ff.

25. See A. von Harnack, *Christus praesens—Vicarius Christi* (Sitzungsberichte der Berliner Akademie der Wissenschaften, 1927, Nr. 34), esp. pp. 434f. Albert Hauck, *Der Gedanke der päpstlichen Weltherrschaft bis auf Bonifaz VIII* (Leipzig, 1904), had pointed out how the papal claim to preeminence of the spiritual over against all secular powers, which was present since the Carolingian period, was changed by Pope Gregory VII into a claim to *principalis potestas* because Christ supposedly had placed Peter above all the kingdoms of the world (p. 25). Bernard of Clairvaux, then, was the first to interpret the "two swords" of Luke 22:38 in terms of the secular and the spiritual power, both being handed over to the church *(ibid.).* For Innocent III, see *ibid.,* pp. 36f.

26. For the following, see Percy E. Schramm, *Der König von Frankreich* (1939; 2d ed., Darmstadt, 1960), esp. pp. 30f., 32ff., 42f.

27. Schramm, pp. 181, 184f.

28. Schramm, p. 228.

29. Hans Kohn, *Die Idee des Nationalismus. Ursprung und Geschichte bis zur französischen Revolution* (Heidelberg, 1950), p. 805.

30. Kohn, p. 840.

31. Oliver Cromwell, *The Writings and Speeches of Oliver Cromwell,* with Introd., Notes, and a Sketch of His Life by Wilbur Cortez Abbott (Russell & Russell, 1970), Vol. III, p. 63.

32. *Ibid.,* Vol. IV, pp. 27f.

33. For quotations, see Kohn, p. 247.

34. John Milton, *Selected Prose,* ed. by C. A. Patrides (Penguin Books, 1947), p. 279.

35. *Ibid.,* p. 236.

36. *Ibid.,* p. 238.

37. Quoted from Robert N. Bellah, "Civil Religion in America," *Daedalus,* 1967, p. 13.

38. Richard J. Neuhaus, *Time Toward Home: The American Experiment as Revelation* (Seabury Press, 1975), p. 72.

39. Arnold J. Toynbee, *A Study of History* (Oxford University Press, 1960), pp. 8f., 10.

40. *Ibid.,* p. 3.

41. It is the view that goes back to E. Durkheim and is represented today

in the first place by Talcott Parsons and his school, in Germany by Thomas Luckmann and N. Luhmann. For a discussion of the implicit problems of this approach in the form of a comparative analysis of N. Luhmann and J. Habermas, see T. Rendtorff, *Gesellschaft ohne Religion?* (Munich, 1975).

42. See Eric Voegelin, *Israel and Revelation*, Vol. I of Order and History (1955), p. ix: "The order of history is the history of order." In his discussion with Toynbee, pp. 116ff., Voegelin raises, concerning the history of Israel, objections of a similar kind as have been raised here in relation to Toynbee's concept of Western culture.

43. The recent historical discussion on the "crisis of the seventeenth century" suggests that this period rather than the Renaissance or the Reformation constitutes the watershed from which the modern period emerged. Although earlier developments contributed to the changes of the seventeenth century toward a secularized form of society, those tendencies became definitive only with the impasse of the confessional wars. Theodore K. Rabb, *The Struggle for Stability in Early Modern Europe* (Oxford University Press, 1975), argues that the epochal change of that century in people's attitude toward authority (p. 33) was due primarily to "the effects of war," especially to those of the Thirty Years' War in Germany (pp. 119ff.), essentially connected with "the decline of religion as a stimulus to violence" (p. 80).